Liturgies for Weddings

Flor McCarthy

Drawings by
Pauline McGrath

DOMINICAN PUBLICATIONS

First published (2006) by
Dominican Publications
42 Parnell Square
Dublin 1

ISBN 1-871552-99-0

British Library Cataloguing in Publications Data.
A catalogue record for this book is available
from the British Library.

Cover design by Bill Bolger

Printed by
The Leinster Leader Ltd
Naas
Co. Kildare

Contents

Foreword for celebrants

The majority of couples walk down the aisle feeling optimistic and hopeful. We must not throw cold water on their idealism. We have to tread softly because we are treading on their dreams. Nevertheless, it ought to be possible to introduce a little realism by hinting at the patient work and willing sacrifice required if their hopes are to be realised.

Today great emphasis is placed on marriage as a relationship, and rightly so. And in the eyes of the Church, when a couple get married they take an irreversible step. From that day forward their lives and destinies are inextricably bound up with one another. This is a huge commitment to make.

Marriage as a deep and loving relationship, the irreversible nature of the step taken, and the depth of the commitment involved – these are some of the topics which are emphasised in these liturgies.

The wedding ceremony is very important. The task of making it special lies chiefly with the celebrant. Here the Scripture readings have a vital role to play. The Word of God powerfully illuminates the nature and meaning of marriage. It is customary nowadays for the couple to choose the Scripture readings. This is good, but the average couple may need a little guidance. (See *Foreword for couples*, pp. 8-9).

For many celebrants the homily is their main, if not only, concern. The homily is important because it gives us a chance to talk about the heart of the Gospel - God's love for us and our love for one another. But the rest of the ceremony is important too. Hence, I have provided wedding liturgies rather than just wedding homilies.

The heart of the ceremony is the exchange of vows. We must do our utmost to solemnise this moment. And it must be clear that the couple are the ministers of the sacrament.

Sometimes the ceremony includes the celebration of the Eucharist, and sometimes it doesn't. Both circumstances are catered for in the book.

Four liturgies for wedding anniversaries are also provided, as well as a formula for the renewal of the wedding vows. Each liturgy is followed by two short reflective pieces. Some of these summarise the main point of the homily; others offer a new insight.

Weddings provide a marvellous pastoral opportunity. We should be positive in what we say. And we should be as kind and helpful as possible to the couple lest we dim in the slightest way the joy of this unique day in their lives.

Foreword for couples

In our times many of the traditional external supports of marriage have disappeared. Today the partners have to fall back on their own innate strengths, and their own capacity for faithfulness. We all pine for human warmth, closeness, and love. However, these things cannot be got from shallow and transient attachments, but only from deep and lasting relationships.

Marriage as a deep and loving relationship, the irreversible nature of the step taken, and the depth of the commitment involved, are some of the topics emphasised in these liturgies.

As your wedding day approaches you will have many things to think about. The most important of these is the wedding ceremony. This book is meant to help you plan that ceremony.

Here the Scripture readings have a vital role to play. The Word of God powerfully illuminates the nature and meaning of marriage. It is your prerogative to choose the scripture readings. This book provides a rich and varied menu to choose from. The normal practice is to have three readings.

The *first reading is* taken from the Old Testament. This is followed by a psalm (unless a hymn is substituted). The *second reading is* taken from the New Testament. The *third reading* comes the Gospel. Just before the Gospel comes a brief verse referred to as the *Gospel Acclamation.*

In choosing the readings I offer the following piece of guidance. One reading might deal with the divine origin of marriage, and one or both of the other two with the importance of love in the Christian life. The book contains three examples of the first: A1, A2, and E4. The best examples of the second are: C2, C4, C5, C7, and E6. There are thirteen liturgies in this book, each with its own theme. I have suggested some specific reading or readings to go along with a particular theme. You might keep that in mind when making your choices.

Each liturgy is followed by two short reflective pieces. Some of these summarise the main point of the homily; others offer a new insight.

Remember that it is not the celebrant but you who are the ministers of the sacrament. Sometimes the ceremony includes the celebration of the Eucharist, and sometimes it doesn't. Both circumstances are catered for in the book.

As for the music, hymns are more appropriate than secular songs. Hymns emphasise the religious character of the ceremony.

Keep this book. You might want to turn to it at some point in the future for insight and inspiration.

Flor McCarthy

Note on suggested readings

In each of the seventeen liturgies in this work, there is a section marked 'Suggested Reading(s)', in which one, or, at times, two of the readings found in the *Scripture readings* section (pp. 123-142) is indicated. This is the reading which most closely expresses the theme for that liturgy. The suggestion is that this passage should be among the readings for the liturgy, and that it should be accompanied by two other readings and a psalm – chosen by the couple in conjunction with the celebrant.

Liturgies

I

Where love is, God is

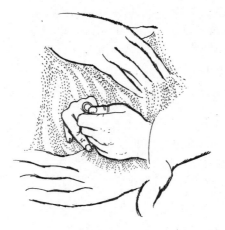

Love of self
Love is the way to God

Introduction

In the name of the Father and of the Son and of the Holy Spirit.

The grace of our Lord Jesus Christ, the love of God, and the fellowship of the Holy Spirit be with you all.

Today N. and N. come before God and this community to

declare their love for each other, and to seal that love in the sacrament of marriage.

We've all experienced the limitations of human love. Therefore, it would be easy to be cynical about love. Still, how bleak life would be without it. And St John tells us that where genuine love is present, God is present.

Wedding Ceremony without Mass

Let us reflect for a moment on the importance of love in human life, and especially in the life of a Christian. [Pause]

Now let us turn to the Lord, who loves us and asks us to love one another.

Opening Prayer

Father, we know that you love us and want us to love one another. Hear our prayers for N. and N., who today are united in marriage. Help them so to love one another that they will always experience your loving presence in their lives. We ask this through Christ our Lord.

Wedding within Mass

Penitential Rite

This is a celebration of love. It is fitting that it takes place in the context of the Eucharist, because the Eucharist is a celebration of God's love for us in Christ. We don't find love easy because we are wounded by selfishness. Let us reflect for a moment on our failure to love others as we should. [Pause].

Now let us turn to the Lord who forgives our sins and helps us to love one another.

Lord Jesus, you came to teach us to love God with all our heart and all our soul. Lord, have mercy.

You came to teach us to love our neighbour as ourselves. Christ, have mercy.

You came to teach us that these two commandments sum up the whole of religion. Lord, have mercy.

May almighty God have mercy on us, forgive us our sins, and bring us to everlasting life.

Opening Prayer
As above

Suggested Reading
C7, p. 136.

Homily

It has been found that when circumstances are very difficult (as for example in a prisoner of war camp) those who live for someone else have a better chance of surviving than those who live only for themselves. The explanation for this lies in the fact that love brings out the best in people. Love is the most powerful force in the world. It awakens in us energies and resources we never knew were there. Love warms the soul, energies the spirit, and supplies passion to life.

Once in a certain kingdom lived two men who made a vow to be friends till death. 'Nothing will ever part us,' they declared. Splendid words, yet easily said. The question was: did they really mean them?

Well, those fine words were soon put to the test. One of them was arrested, accused of being involved in subversive activities. What did the other do? Without a moment's hesitation, he came to the aid of his friend, and insisted on taking the blame himself. The result was that both were brought to trial. They remained loyal to one another in court, so that the judge was hopelessly confused.

The case attracted nation-wide attention. Eventually it reached the ears of the king. He ordered the two men to be brought before him.

'We're for it now,' said one friend to the other. However, they were in for a delightful surprise. Amazed at finding such courage and loyalty among his subjects, the king received them warmly. He said to them, 'You've nothing to worry about. I'm going to set you both free. But before I do, I have a favour to ask of you.'

'What favour could two poor men do for a king?' one of them

asked in astonishment.

'I want you to take me as the third partner in your friendship,' the king replied. The two friends were only too happy to agree to the king's surprising request.

Here we see two people who sealed their friendship with a solemn vow. No one forced them to make that vow. It sprang entirely from the pure and unselfish love they had for one another. And the vow was not just a matter of words. They were prepared to back it up with deeds, indeed with their lives if necessary.

What those two friends did was truly extraordinary. Yet what N. and N. are doing today is no less extraordinary. In pledging their love in marriage, they are making a solemn vow to be true to one another till death. They are doing so of their own free will. Why do they make this vow? Because they love each other, and want to seal their love forever.

Love is the most important thing in life. People might be very successful, and accumulate a lot of money and possessions, and yet be a failure at the most important thing of all, which is to be a loving person. St Paul says, 'If I have no love in me, I am nothing.'

You can't put it more forcefully than that.

Love comes from God. St John says that God is love. It follows that where love is, God is. Hence, when two people commit themselves to one another in love, God commits himself to them. God becomes their partner.

The solemn pledge of love which N. and N. are about to make to each other, and which will be sealed in the sacrament of matrimony, is as yet largely a matter of words. These words will have to be translated into deeds, because their pledge is certain to be tested in the course of their life together. And if they have any weaknesses, and who hasn't?, these will be exposed. But God is their partner in the adventure of love. Let them remember this, and have recourse to God when things are difficult.

Love in the richest sense doesn't fall into our lap like manna from heaven. It is something that we must learn. Christian love draws its inspiration from the words of Jesus: 'Love one another as I have loved you.'

This is a red-letter day for N. and N. God blesses their love and wants it to bear fruit, fruit that will last.

Prayer of the Faithful

President God is love. Those who live in love live in God, and God lives in them. Therefore, let us pray for the gift of true love.

Response Lord, hear our prayer.

Reader(s) For all the followers of Christ: that they may be witnesses to his love by the concern they show for one another. [Pause] Let us pray to the Lord.

For world leaders: that they may work without ceasing to build a more just and peaceful world. [Pause] Let us pray to the Lord.

For N. and N.: that their lives may be an example of partnership, fidelity and love. [Pause] Let us pray to the Lord.

That each may find in the other a true and faithful friend. [Pause] Let us pray to the Lord.

For all here present: that no matter what our state in life, we may be people who are capable of a true and faithful love of others. [Pause] Let us pray to the Lord.

For the lonely and the unloved: that they may find comfort and support. [Pause] Let us pray to the Lord.

For our departed relatives and friends, especially ... (here we could mention anyone who was related to the bride or groom): that we may one day be reunited with them. [Pause] Let us pray to the Lord.

President God of love and mercy, you are the same yesterday, today, and forever. Help us to have confidence in your unchanging love for us, so that when things are difficult, we may have the strength to persevere in the way of love. We ask this through Christ our Lord.

Blessing

May you be poor in misfortune, and rich in blessings.

May you be slow to make enemies, and quick to make friends.

May you get all your wishes but one so you will always have something to strive for.

Reflection – LOVE OF SELF

The Bible says:
'You must love your neighbour *as yourself*.'
Only when we learn to love ourselves,
will we be able to love other people.
Those who are filled with self-loathing
are not going to be able to love others.
They will project those feelings onto others.
They will blame and castigate others
for what they do not like in themselves.

But there is an idea that love of self is wrong.
There is a form of self-love which is wrong.
We call it selfishness or egotism.
But there is a form of self-love which is healthy,
and without which we cannot truly love others.
We can't offer warmth to others
if our own fireplace is cold and empty.
We can only love with the amount of love that is in us.

Whether we are conscious of it or not,
we do love others precisely *as we love ourselves*.
Hence, it is very important
to have a healthy love for ourselves.
That is where love starts.
But of course it is not meant to end there.
All true love of self overflows
in the form of love of others and of God.

Reflection – LOVE IS THE WAY TO GOD

A young disciple who was having doubts came to the Master and said: 'Do you believe in God?'

'Yes, I do,' the Master answered.

The disciple then asked: 'On what evidence do you believe?'

'I believe in God because I know him,' came the reply. 'I experience his presence in me twenty-four hours of every day.'

'But how is this possible?' the disciple asked.

'Where love is, God is,' the master replied. 'When we love, we experience God, and doubt vanishes like mist before the sun,' replied the Master.

The disciple thought for a while, then asked: 'How can I achieve this kind of certainty?'

'By acts of love,' the Master replied. 'Try to love your neighbours; love them actively and unceasingly. And as you learn to love them more and more, you will become more and more convinced of the existence of God and the immortality of the soul. This has been tested. This is the true way.'

Darkness came down, and then
I doubted all;
And there was no one in the lonely glen
To hear my call.
I doubted God, and I doubted
My secret soul;
The legions of Heaven were routed
And I had no goal.
I doubted Beauty and Love
And wandered forth
A child of despair, to rove
The faithless earth.
And then like an angel she came;
I ceased to rove;
In her heart was a pure white flame
And she was love.

Patrick Kavanagh

2

A *sacrament of love*

Love is well-being
Giving and receiving

Introduction

In the name of the Father and of the Son and of the Holy Spirit.

The grace of our Lord Jesus Christ, the love of God, and the fellowship of the Holy Spirit be with you all.

Welcome to the wedding ceremony of N. and N. During this ceremony they will commit themselves to love one another for life. Nothing provides a greater challenge to love, or offers such opportunities for its practice, as marriage. Marriage is rooted and grounded in love. A marriage without love is like a flower garden without flowers.

Wedding Ceremony without Mass

But true and genuine love does not come easy to us. We need the Holy Spirit to touch our hearts so that we can love unselfishly. Let us reflect on this for a moment. [Pause]

Opening Prayer

Almighty and ever-living God, we know it is your will that we should love one another. But we also know that without your help we are unable to love as we should. Look with kindness on N. and N., who today are united in marriage before your altar. Grant that the Holy Spirit may warm their hearts and strengthen their wills so that they may be capable of true and lasting love. We ask this through Christ our Lord.

Wedding within Mass

Penitential Rite

Jesus said, 'Love one another as I have loved you.' Of all the commandments he gave us, this is the most important. The greatest failure in the life of a disciple of Jesus is the failure to love. Let us reflect for a moment on the fact that we do not always love others as we should. [Pause]

Let us now confess our sins, especially our failure to live the commandment of love.

I confess to almighty God ...

May almighty God have mercy on us, forgive us our sins, and bring us to everlasting life.

Opening Prayer
As above

Suggested Reading
C2, p. 133.

Homily

Marriage is a sacrament of love. If there is one word that could sum up love it is surely the word 'giving'. Giving can take many forms. But the giving we are concerned with here is not so much the giving of *things* but the giving of *oneself*. We give but little when we give of our possessions. It is when we give of ourselves that we truly give.

However, we tend to see giving as depriving ourselves of something. It is true that some givers are impoverished through giving; they experience a sense of loss, because they give grudgingly. But others are enriched as they give; far from experiencing a sense of loss, their hearts are enlarged, because they give joyfully.

There is a famous parable which goes like this. One day a poor man was sitting by the side of the road begging. But at the end of the morning he had nothing to show for his efforts. Weary and dejected, he continued to sit there in the hot noon sun. By his side lay a sack which contained a handful of wheat grains, just enough to make one last cake of bread.

Suddenly he saw the king's carriage approaching. 'The king is a kind man. He will surely give me something,' the beggarman said to himself, as he got to his feet. To his delight the royal carriage began to slow down and came to a halt directly opposite the spot where he stood with outstretched hand.

Down came the window, and the king put his head out. The beggarman bowed low and was about to say, 'Your Majesty, could you spare a little money for me, your most unworthy servant?' But the king got in the first words. Reaching out his hand towards the beggarman he said, 'Friend, could you spare a little corn for your king?'

Completely taken aback, the beggarman said, 'Certainly, your Majesty.' With that he opened the sack, picked out the smallest grain of wheat he could find, and gave it to the king. The king thanked him, and the carriage moved off, leaving the beggarman with a terrible feeling of emptiness and disappointment.

All day long he sat there begging but got nothing. When evening came on he made his way home, tired, hungry, and dejected. Once home, he took a pan and emptied the last of the wheat from the sack into it. As he inspected the meagre heap of grains, he made a startling discovery - the smallest grain had turned into a grain of pure gold. Then he bitterly regretted that he had been so miserly with his king.

The moral of the parable: it is by giving that we receive, it is by sharing that we are enriched. The moral is important for everyone, but especially for those entering marriage. Nothing provides such opportunities for giving as does marriage. However, some enter marriage with the mentality of a beggar. They are concerned about what their partner can do for them rather than what they can do for their partner. They want to receive, but not to give.

Of course, we all need to receive. There is no such thing as a completely self-sufficient individual. Some find it hard to receive for fear of appearing inadequate. Others find it hard to receive because they don't want to be dependent on others. It is tragic not to be able to receive. Just as the parched earth soaks in the rain, so we must not be afraid to open our parched hearts and soak in the love of others.

But if we only want to receive, and are not willing to give, that too would be tragic. It would mean we are no better than a beggar. It doesn't help that we live in selfish times. 'The prevailing philosophy today is: everything must be grabbed from life immediately and with both hands' (Solzhenitsyn).

Love is a beautiful thing, but it easily becomes tainted by self-interest. In a recent poll a number of people were asked, 'Why do you want to get married?' Almost all replied, 'To be loved.' One fears for marriages that begin like that. If being loved is our goal we will fail to achieve it. If we expect another person to make us happy, we will be endlessly disappointed. On the other hand, when you have a couple who are willing to give as well as to receive, there is great hope for their marriage.

Giving doesn't have to involve big deeds. Small deeds are very important. They may not look much, but they accumulate to create a friendly atmosphere. Small flowers give off little scent on their own, but put a bunch of them together and they can fill a room with fragrance.

Through giving one becomes a loving person. Loving involves risk. To love is to open one's heart, and to open one's heart is to become vulnerable. We can be hurt if our love is not returned. But those who opt for love, open themselves to the possibilities of a greater happiness than they have ever known.

Love is well-being. Love makes us fruitful. To refuse to love is to begin to die. To begin to love is to begin to live. Love calls on us to cultivate the fullness and depth of who we are.

N. and N. are about to pledge their love for one another in the sacrament of matrimony. Marriage draws its strength from God, who is the source of love. May the Lord help them to love one another in such a way that they will reach their full potential as human beings and as his precious children.

Prayer of the Faithful

President: God sent his Son among us to give us an example of unselfish love, and to remind us that our true vocation in life is to be loving people. Let us pray for the ability to love.

Response: Lord, hear us in your love.

Reader(s): For the Church: that it may never forget the primacy of love, and never tire of encouraging its members to love one another. [Pause] We pray in faith.

For world leaders: that they may work untiringly to build a world free from poverty and oppression, so that all peoples may be able to live in freedom and dignity. [Pause] We pray in faith.

For N. and N., who have committed themselves to one another in love: that the Lord may keep them true and faithful to one another. [Pause] We pray in faith.

That they may be able to give to one another with generosity, and to receive from one another with thankfulness. [Pause] We pray in faith.

For those who do not know how to love because they never received love. [Pause] We pray in faith.

For those who have died, especially ... (here we could mention anyone who was related to the bride or groom): that the Lord's eternal love may shine brightly on them. [Pause] We pray in faith.

President: All-powerful God, you know our weakness. May we reach out with trust to grasp your hand so that we may walk joyfully and courageously in the way of love. We ask this through Christ our Lord.

Blessing

May you know the joy that springs up in the hearts of those who say 'yes' to love.

May you know the sweetness that falls like dew into the hearts of those who treat others kindly.

And may the Lord bless your home with the laughter of children.

Reflection – LOVE IS WELL-BEING

Once a lonely, unloved child was sitting by a wall when a toad emerged from a nearby cave. The child quickly took out her silk scarf — the kind which toads love to walk on — and spread it out before him. As soon as the toad saw the scarf he went back into the cave, and soon returned carrying a little crown of gold which he placed on the scarf. Then he went into the cave again.

On seeing the glittering crown, the child's eyes lit up with desire. She grabbed it and put it in her pocket. Soon the toad came out again, but when he didn't see the crown on the scarf, he crept over to the wall, and from sheer sorrow at discovering that he had been robbed of his treasure, beat his little head against the wall until he fell dead.

That child didn't love the toad. She exploited him. She acted not only very selfishly but also very foolishly, because had she been patient, and let the crown lie where it was, she would have had the joy of watching the toad bring out more of his treasures from the cave.

Sometimes when two people fall in love
they desire rather than love each other.
Desire is only a starting point.
Love goes beyond desire.
Those who stop at desire will never know love.
When they have taken all they want,
they will begin to look elsewhere
for another desire and another fulfilment.
Some people enter a relationship
with the mentality of a beggar:
they want to receive all the time.
But others have a more mature attitude.
They know they need to receive,
but they also know they need to give.
In giving they discover their own wealth,
and experience a feeling of being alive,
just as a tree does in springtime,
when offering its buds and blossoms to the world.
Love is well-being.
To open one's heart is to begin to live;
to close one's heart is to begin to die.

Reflection – GIVING AND RECEIVING

In a relationship there must be a continuous interplay
between giving and receiving.

Giving is very important because it is
through giving that the heart remains open.
But this giving has to have a certain quality.
Sadly, much of our giving is tainted by self-interest.
Some give but only on condition
that they receive something in return.
This is really self-giving.
But others give without expecting anything in return.
Some givers are impoverished as they give,
because they give grudgingly.
But others are enriched as they give,

because they give joyfully.
It is not so much about giving *things*
as about giving of *ourselves*.
We give but little when we give of our possessions.
It is when you give of ourselves that we truly give.

Receiving is also very important.
However, some find it hard to receive
for fear of appearing inadequate.
Others find it hard to receive
because they don't want to be dependent on others.
But we all need to receive.
There is no such thing as a self-sufficient individual.
It is nothing short of tragic not to be able to receive.
Hence, it is not enough to know how to give.
We must also know how to receive.
When we receive with graciousness
we do wonders for the giver.
We give him/her a chance
to enter the world of sharing.

When we give cheerfully, and receive gratefully,
everyone is blessed.

3
The lamp of love

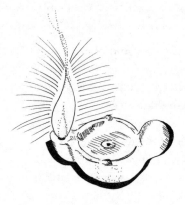

Tending the lamp
The problem of love

This liturgy involves the use of three candles, two small ones and one large one. The small candles stand for the love which each of the partners brings to the marriage. The large candle stands for the 'lamp' of their married love which is put on public display on this day. The couple light the two small candles at the start of the ceremony. They light the large one after they have exchanged their vows. This is a very simple ritual yet it can communicate powerfully.

Introduction

In the name of the Father and of the Son and of the Holy Spirit. The grace of our Lord Jesus Christ, the love of God, and the fellowship of the Holy Spirit be with you all.

I welcome you to this Mass (ceremony) during which N. and N. will make their wedding vows. This is a bright day for them, and for their families. It is a day of joy for all of us gathered here. I now invite each of them to light a candle. (They do this).

Light is a symbol of love. Without love the world would be very dark place. Thanks to the love of N. and N., a new lamp shines in our midst.

Wedding Ceremony without Mass

But we know that the lamp of human love is a frail one, and can grow dim or even go out altogether. The one lamp that never goes out or grows dim is the lamp of God's love for us. Let us reflect on this for a moment. [Pause]

Let us now turn to God, and call down his blessing on N. and N., and on all gathered here.

Opening Prayer

Almighty and eternal God, to live in love is to live in the light. Let the light of your love shine brightly on N. and N., who today are being united in the sacrament of marriage. May their love be an unwavering flame that will bring them safely through the shadows of this world to the radiant glory of your kingdom. We ask this through Christ our Lord.

Wedding Ceremony within Mass

Penitential Rite

As Christians, all of us, no matter what our state in life, are called to be loving people. Anyone who is a truly loving person is living in the light. Anyone who is not a loving person is living in darkness. Let us reflect on this for a moment. [Pause]

It is the Lord himself who helps us to walk in the light.

Lord Jesus, through the light of faith you help us to banish the darkness of doubt and unbelief. Lord, have mercy.

Through the light of hope you help us to banish the darkness of sadness and despair. Christ, have mercy.

Through the light of love you help us to banish the darkness of selfishness and hatred. Lord, have mercy.

May almighty God have mercy on us, forgive us our sins, and bring us to everlasting life.

Opening Prayer
as above

Suggested Readings
C6, p. 136. E2, p. 139.

Homily

Light is a wonderful thing in itself. But it is also a powerful symbol. In this ceremony we are using it as a symbol of love.

The word 'love' has become somewhat devalued in our times. Therefore, it would be easy to be cynical about it. This would be a tragedy because love is as necessary for us as light. In fact, it is a special kind of light. Without love the world would be a very dark place. Love lights up everything. It brings hope to a world darkened by selfishness, indifference and hatred.

Those who love shed light around them because love makes everything bright. To see such people is to see human beings at their best and brightest. They are like a lamp alight and shining.

St John says that God is love. This is the most important thing the Bible has to say about God. And the most important thing the Bible has to say about ourselves is that we are make in God's image. This means that each of us has an innate capacity to love. The image of God is at its best and brightest in us when we love. When we love we become like God.

Each of us is capable of shedding some light around us. Few of us can aspire to be a beacon which sheds light far and wide. But all of us are capable of being a candle which sheds light into its own immediate environment.

I've no doubt but that N. and N. have a lot of love in them. The two (small) candles they lit earlier stand for their individual loves. For some time now these lights have been burning quietly in our midst. But soon they will take their individual candles and with them they will light the large candle. In this way, (just as Jesus wished), they are placing the lamp of their love on a lamp-stand. Thus it will give light, not only to them, but also to their families, to their friends, to the community, and to an extent to all the world.

Thanks to technology, we now have lamps that never go out. The human lamp, however, is not so reliable. It needs constant tending. How do we keep this lamp burning? Through a continuous input of small drops of oil. What do these drops of oil consist of? They are the small things of daily life, the little words and deeds of kindness and of service. These are the drops that keep the flame of love alive in our hearts.

But N. and N. will need the help of God in order to love one another with constancy and generosity. God showed his love for us when he sent his Son, Jesus, into the world. Jesus is 'the light of the world', a light no darkness can overpower. To those who believe in him and follow him he made a marvellous promise. He promised that they would never walk in darkness but would always have the light of life.

I encourage N. and N. to have faith in Christ and in his love for them. He will show them the way and lead them forward.

Prayer of the Faithful

President We have lifted up the lamp of love and placed it on the lamp-stand so that it can give light to all here present. Let us turn to God and ask his blessing on us all, and especially on N. and N.

Response Lord, let your light shine on us.

Reader(s) For the Church: that through its ministry the light of the Gospel may shine for all the world to see. [Pause] Let us pray to the Lord.

For the world in which we live, a world darkened by war: that the light of peace may shine on it. [Pause] Let

27

us pray to the Lord..

For N. and N. : that they may walk always in the light of true and faithful love. [Pause] Let us pray to the Lord.

That they may know God's help in times of weakness, so that they may not stumble or lose their way. [Pause] Let us pray to the Lord.

For those who have never known in their lives the warmth and brightness of love. [Pause] Let us pray to the Lord.

For all here present: that this celebration may encourage us to persevere in the way of love. [Pause] Let us pray to the Lord.

For our departed loved ones, especially ... (here we could mention anyone who was related to the bride or groom): that the light of heaven may shine on them. [Pause] Let us pray to the Lord.

President: God of mercy, save us from the darkness of broken promises. Help us to walk in the light of faithful love, and in your goodness bring us to your kingdom of everlasting light. We ask this through Christ our Lord.

Blessing

May the Lord save you from the darkness of broken promises, and enable you to walk in the light of faithful love.

When the darkness of sorrow falls, may you remember that you never walk alone.

And when you have passed through the shadows of this world, may the Lord bring you to his kingdom of everlasting light.

Reflection – TENDING THE LAMP

Light is a symbol of love.
In fact, love is a special kind of light.
Love makes everything bright.
Without the light of love

the world would be a very dark place.
Those who love shed light around them.
They are like a radiant lamp.
Thanks to technology,
we now have lamps that never go out.
The human lamp, however,
hasn't changed much over the centuries.
It is still a frail and imperfect thing.
This is so because we have within us
a certain amount of darkness.
Our innate selfishness dims the lamp of love.
Besides, there are outside forces
which conspire to extinguish it.
Hence, if we want the lamp to keep on burning
we must tend it diligently
How do we tend this precious lamp?
Through a continuous input of small drops of oil.
What do these drops of oil consist of?
They are the small things of daily life,
the little words and deeds of kindness and of service.

Reflection – THE PROBLEM OF LOVE

A man thinks that if he is successful, he is assured of love. And a woman thinks that if she is beautiful, she is assured of love. But in practice it doesn't work out like that. Some of the world's most successful men and the world's most beautiful women are among the loneliest people on earth.

Marylin Monroe was one of the most glamorous women in the history of Hollywood. Towards the end of her life, she said to her maid, Lena, 'Nobody's ever going to love me now. And I don't blame them. What am I good for? I can't have children. I can't cook. I've been divorced three times. Who would want me?'

'Oh, lots of men would want you,' Lena replied.

'Yes,' said Marylin, 'lots of men would *want* me. But who would *love* me?'

Sadly, the answer was probably 'nobody'.

Many people see the problem of love
as *being loved* rather than *being a loving person*.
They try their hardest to make themselves loveable
through being successful, or glamorous, or rich.
And so they end up without love,
because they are loved, not for themselves,
but for something they possess or have achieved.
Whereas if they became loving people,
they would be loved for themselves.
We all crave to be loved for ourselves.

There are three states:
Not to love and not to be loved;
this seems like hell on earth.
To love but not to be loved in return;
this, though painful, is better than the first.
To love and to be loved; this is the best.

4
When the wine runs out

When romantic love fades
Weeds among the wheat

Introduction

In the name of the Father and of the Son and of the Holy Spirit.

The grace of our Lord Jesus Christ, the love of God, and the fellowship of the Holy Spirit be with you all.

Water is a great thing. Without it there would be no life on earth. Yet no one in his right mind would compare it to wine. Strictly speaking we could survive without wine, but life would be the poorer for its absence.

At a wedding in Cana Jesus changed water into excellent wine. He is present with us today as we celebrate the wedding of N. and N. We pray that he will enable them to give and receive the wine of love.

Wedding Ceremony without Mass

Let us pause for a moment in order to enliven our faith in the presence of the Lord among us. [Pause]

Opening Prayer

God of power and love, hear our prayers for N. and N., who today are celebrating their marriage. May Christ who brought joy to a wedding at Cana be present with them today and throughout their married lives. When the wine of their love is found wanting, may he touch their hearts with his grace, so that they may taste the new wine of unselfish love. We ask this through the same Christ our Lord.

Wedding within Mass

Penitential Rite

Let us reflect for a moment on the quality of the love we share with others. [Pause] Let us ask the Lord to help us to be loving people.

Lord Jesus, you help us to change the water of doubt into the wine of faith. Lord, have mercy.

You help us to change the water of despair into the wine of hope. Christ, have mercy.

You help us the change the water of selfishness into the wine of love. Lord, have mercy.

May almighty God have mercy on us, forgive us our sins, and bring us to everlasting life.

Opening Prayer
As above

Suggested Reading
E5, p. 141.

Homily

What happened at the wedding at Cana happens sooner or later in every marriage, namely, the wine runs out. What do we mean by this?

Hardly any enterprise creates such high expectations as marriage. The typical marriage starts off with a feast of joy. The couple are surrounded by friends and well-wishers who shower them with gifts. Full of hopes and dreams, they set off on their honeymoon. The wine is flowing freely.

They come back from the honeymoon and the real business begins – setting up a home and learning to live with one another. At first they find great joy in each other's company. They are convinced that their love was pre-ordained in heaven and meant to last for eternity. It looks as if their expectations are going to be fulfilled. The wine is still flowing.

But when human beings are close to one another problems inevitably occur. As the partners get to know one another, they discover that they didn't marry an angel after all, but an imperfect human being, with the same needs and failings as themselves. (It is said that you fall in love with someone by choosing who you wish they were, but then find out who they really are).

Everything is so different from what they expected. The honeymoon is over. The wine has run out. What are they to do? Some may be tempted to run out with the wine, declaring: 'There's nothing in it for me any longer.' For some people marriage is only a passing alliance of two selfish human beings. So, when they have taken all they can from each other, they look elsewhere for more fruit that can be picked and eaten without pain or effort.

But what can a couple do?

The first thing is not to panic or despair. They must face the fact that the first wine has run out.

The second thing is to beware of looking for false substitutes. They must resist the temptation to abandon the relationship and lose themselves in a career or a hectic social life.

The third thing is to work on their relationship. If they do this, they will grow as persons and discover the real meaning of love. In this way the crisis can become an opportunity.

Here is a surprising thing: it is necessary that the first wine should run out. Otherwise the new wine can't come in. The first wine stands for first love, or romantic love, as it's called. Romantic love is not an aberration. It is a powerful taste of the divine. But it doesn't last. However, this is not a tragedy. In fact, it is a necessity. It has to wear out so that a new and deeper love can be born.

Love transcends feelings. The new love is typified by Mary's attitude at Cana – 'they have no wine'. It consists in putting the other person before ourselves. This new love goes deeper than the oscillations of one's feelings and moods. It means learning to love the real person and not some idealised self-projection.

Love is a difficult adventure. To enter marriage is to enter a school of love, a school in which all are slow learners. It requires a lot of effort to go from a desire to receive to a desire to give. It is impossible to unaided human nature. This is why, like the couple of Cana, we need the presence of Christ.

The changing of water into wine symbolises what Jesus' ministry was about. He changed beyond recognition the lives of those who came into contact with him. And he continues to do this for those who believe in him and follow him. He offers us something that we pine for but can't achieve on our own. He offers us a share in the divine life of God. He brings a joy which the world cannot give.

The new wine is meant not just for married couples but for everyone. The new wine cannot be put into old wineskins. This means we have to change. The Holy Spirit has to touch our hearts so that we can love unselfishly.

When N. and N. come up against their limitations let them turn to Christ. For those who seek his help, the miracle of Cana still happens – the water of selfishness is turned into the wine of true love. And good as the old wine was, the new wine is better.

Prayer of the Faithful

President Jesus brought joy to a young couple and their guests at Cana by turning water into wine. Let us bring our needs before him with confidence.

Response: Lord, hear us in your love.

Reader(s) For the Pope, the bishops, and all who minister in the Church: that they may see themselves as agents of Christ's love and compassion. [Pause] We pray in faith.

For all who hold public office in society: that they may be instruments of justice and peace. [Pause] We pray in faith.

For N. and N.: that they may know the presence of Christ in their married life, so that they may be able to change the water of selfishness into the wine of true love. [Pause] We pray in faith.

For all married couples: that Christ may help them to persevere when they experience difficulties. [Pause] We pray in faith.

For those who have never known the wine of love in their lives: that they too may experience the blessings of love. [Pause] We pray in faith.

For the faithful departed, especially ... (here we could mention anyone who was related to the bride or groom): that they may be admitted to the wedding feast of eternal life. [Pause] We pray in faith.

President God of love and mercy, may we experience your Son's presence in our lives, so that when our own efforts are not enough, he may support us with his grace. We ask this through the same Christ our Lord.

Blessing

May the Holy Spirit touch your hearts so that you may share with one another the wine of unselfish love.

May the Lord, who brought joy to the young couple at Cana, bless your home with the laughter of children.

And after a long and happy life here on earth, may the Lord give you a place at the wedding feast of heaven.

Reflection – WHEN ROMANTIC LOVE FADES

To the gardener it seemed that winter would never end. But then one morning he went out into his orchard to find the sun shining, birds singing, and blossoms everywhere. Overnight the world had turned into a wonderland. He was intoxicated with joy.

Alas, the magic didn't last. The blossoms soon faded and fell to the ground. Though saddened, the gardener didn't despair; the year was young and things were growing. Then on another morning he went out, and under the leaves, he saw tiny apples beginning to take shape. Once again his heart was filled with joy.

First love, or romantic love, is like springtime.
It is a time of wonder and magic.
It is a powerful taste of the divine.
But it doesn't last.
However, this is not a tragedy.
In fact, it is a necessity.
Romantic love has to wear out
so that a new and deeper love can be born,
just as the blossoms have to die
so that the fruit can come.
This new love goes deeper
than the oscillations of one's feelings and moods.
Love in the richest sense doesn't fall into our lap;
it is something that we must learn.
To enter marriage is to enter a school of love,
a school in which all are slow learners.
To love means to move from a desire to receive
to a desire to give.
It means learning to love the real person
and not some idealised self-projection.
Marriage is a sacrament of love,
that draws its strength from God
who is the source of love.
Dear N. and N.,
pray that when the blossoms fade,
your love will continue to grow.
God blesses your love and wants it to bear fruit,

fruit that will last.

Reflection – WEEDS AMONG THE WHEAT

A farmer sowed good seed in his field and then sat back in expectation of a bumper harvest. Soon it looked as if his expectations were going to be fulfilled. A host of sturdy green shoots sprang up. It brought joy to his heart to see them sway in the wind and dance in the sun.

However, one morning he got a terrible shock. He saw weeds growing among the young wheat. He was desperately disappointed, and wanted to rush out and pull up the weeds. But he soon realised that this was not on. In doing so he would pull up some of the wheat too. He was sorely tempted to start all over again with a different field.

However, he eventually calmed down and was able to see things in better perspective. True, there were some weeds in his precious field. But there was excellent wheat there too. He would have to work on the wheat in the hope that it would outgrow the weeds. And that's what he did.

One day he made a discovery which gave him great heart. He noticed that the presence of the weeds was forcing the wheat to reach and strain upwards. In so doing it grew all the better. When the harvest day came, to his delight, a fine harvest resulted. And for some strange reason he got more joy out of reaping that harvest than out of any other.

Something similar happens in every marriage. The partners set out with sky-high expectations. They expect their partner to provide them with continuous friendship and unwavering love. For a while it seems as if their expectations are going to be fulfilled. Living together brings great joy. Each regards the other as perfect.

But time passes and inevitably the weeds appear. They discover that they did not marry an angel after all, but an imperfect human being, with similar needs and failings as themselves. The sooner they accept this situation the better. They must be careful lest the faults they discover in each other blind them to the good that is there too. We help people more by giving them a favourable image of themselves than by constantly harping on their faults.

The road from selfishness to love is a long and difficult one. It begins when the partners accept each other as they are. To love an imperfect human being is a struggle. But it is precisely through this kind of struggle that love grows.

5
Giving one's solemn word

Looking for the ideal partner
Marriage statistics

Introduction

In the name of the Father and of the Son and of the Holy Spirit.

The grace of our Lord Jesus Christ, the love of God, and the fellowship of the Holy Spirit be with you all.

This is truly a fateful day for N. and N. Today they are giving their word irrevocably to one another. We are here to encourage them with our good wishes and to support them with our prayers.

Marriage calls for a profound fidelity. Fidelity demands discipline and sacrifice, things which don't come easy. In truth, only God is fully faithful to his word.

Wedding Ceremony without Mass

Let us turn to God now, and ask him to grant the grace of fidelity to N. and N., and to ourselves. [Pause]

Opening Prayer

Almighty and ever-living God, you are always faithful to us, and guide us in all our decisions. Bless N. and N., who today give their solemn word to be faithful to one another in marriage. Save them from the darkness of broken promises, and help them to walk in the light of faithful love. We ask this through Christ our Lord.

Wedding within Mass

Penitential Rite

Let us now turn to God and ask forgiveness for our infidelities. [Pause]

Lord, you are slow to anger and rich in mercy. Lord, have mercy.

You forgive all our sins, and heal all our ills. Christ, have mercy.

As a father has compassion on his children, so you have compassion on those who revere you. Lord, have mercy.

May almighty God have mercy on us, forgive us our sins, and bring us to everlasting life.

Opening Prayer
As above

Suggested Reading
C2, p. 133.

Homily

'I promise to be true to you in good times and in bad, in sickness and in health. I will love you and honour you all the days of my life.' In a moment N. and N. will speak these (or similar) words to one another.

These are great words, and carry enormous freight. Yet how lightly they trip off the lips. The quality of these words is all-important.

The core quality is that of sincerity. We must mean what we say. To say these words is nothing. To mean them is everything. To mean them is to be prepared to stand over them and to honour them.

One of the greatest things we can give another person is our word. In a sense it is the only thing we have to give that is truly ours. However, it's easy to give our word. It doesn't cost anything there and then. The cost comes later, if and when we honour our word.

A person's word is a great test of his/her character. A person is as good as his word. If that is so, then the question is: How good is my word? At the end of the day what matters is that words are acted on. Fine words are no substitute for fine deeds.

Some people are very generous with their word. They will promise the sun, moon and stars. But they can't be relied on. They don't really mean what they say. Their promises dissolve like salt in water. How painful it is to deal with such people.

But there are other people who are slow to give their word. They don't make promises easily. But when they do make a promise, they can be relied on to honour it. Their promise is like a chain around their leg. How lovely it is to deal with such people.

Marriage promises are the most important promises we are likely to make. Of course, on the wedding day itself, a couple can't know what their promises will demand of them. This will be revealed to them as they go along.

Faithfulness is one of the greatest and most necessary things in life. But it is not easy. If one wishes to be faithful, one must be prepared to put oneself, one's pleasures, comforts, and interests in second place.

Faithfulness is the ability to stick with one's choice. It requires great strength of character. A person's moral greatness consists in the ability to be faithful. However, even though faithfulness is not easy, it brings great rewards. There is no happiness or growth except in the fulfilment of one's obligations. If N. and N. are faithful to their promises, they can expect the greatest measure of happiness a man and woman can have.

There are no such rewards for the unfaithful. There is no happiness at the end of the day for those who give their word but fail to honour it. But there is great joy for those who give their word and keep it.

Today N and N are giving their solemn word to one another. They are giving their word irrevocably. To give one's word irrevocably means there can no going back on it. When they have difficulties, let them remember this moment when they stood here together and exchanged these solemn words.

God looks with love on them today. Through the sacrament of matrimony his grace will be available to them. God is with all those who decide to love each other faithfully. Marriage is a sacrament of love, which draws its strength from God who is the source of love.

Prayer of the Faithful

President   N. and N. have given their solemn word to one another. Let us pray that God will give them the strength to honour that word all the days of their lives.

Response   Lord, graciously hear us.

Reader(s)   For Christians: that their lives may bear witness to the faith they profess with their lips. [Pause] Lord, hear us.

For our political and civil leaders: that they may be faithful to their responsibilities and commitments. [Pause] Lord, hear us.

For N. and N.: that they may be true to the solemn promises they have exchanged. [Pause] Lord, hear us.

That their love for each other may never wilt, but grow stronger as each year goes by. [Pause] Lord, hear us.

For all married couples: that they may remain faithful to one another in spite of difficulties. [Pause] Lord, hear us.

For those who have been the victims of broken promises: that they may find healing and peace. [Pause] Lord, hear us.

For all those who have died, especially ... (here we could mention anyone who was related to the bride or groom): that God may fulfil for them his promise of eternal life. [Pause] Lord, hear us.

President   Lord our God, you are always faithful to your word. Look with kindness on us in our weakness. Grant that what we have said with our lips, we may believe with our hearts, and practise with our lives. We make this prayer through Christ our Lord.

Blessing

May God save you from the darkness of broken promises.
May God enable you to walk in the light of faithful love.
May you know that, no matter what, God will always be faithful to you.

Reflection – LOOKING FOR THE IDEAL PARTNER

Andrew seemed a good candidate for marriage. Yet he had never married. One day a friend said to him, 'Andrew, how come you never got married?'

And Andrew said, 'When I was young I was looking for the perfect woman. Early on I met a girl who seemed to fit the bill. She was intelligent and beautiful, but turned out to be very selfish. So nothing came of that. Later I met another girl. She was well-off and highly educated, but we had nothing in common. The same thing happened a third time. Finally I met a woman who was perfect. She was beautiful, intelligent, generous, everything a man could want.'

'Then why didn't you marry her?' his friend asked.

'She was looking for the perfect man,' Andrew answered.

Those who are looking for the perfect partner
will be looking for ever.
Only God is perfect.
What is it that we most want from a marriage?
To love and to be loved.
To be happy and secure.
To grow together.
To learn to love the real person
and not some idealised self-projection.
We are right to have high expectations of marriage,
but we should not have impossible expectations.
No human being can fully satisfy
the longings of our hearts.
Human love always falls short,
but creates in us a longing for complete love.
Only God can provide us with complete love.
In God all our scattered longings are gathered together.
In the immortal words of St Augustine:
'You made us for yourself, O Lord,
and our hearts will never rest until they rest in you.'

Reflection – MARRIAGE STATISTICS

According to statistics, one out of two marriages in America and Britain ends in divorce. Five main reasons are given for this high failure rate.

1. Real communication between the partners breaks down or ceases altogether.
2. Marriage is understood as a contract that can be broken.
3. The partners develop in different directions; their lives so diverge that they end up as strangers with scarcely anything in common.
4. Sexual and emotional promiscuity becomes the norm.
5. A growing sense of boredom develops.

The above statistics are undoubtedly very negative. However, we can look on them a positive way. They tell us that one out of two marriages succeed. They succeed for the following reasons:

1. Real communication between husband and wife is seen as a skill that can be developed.
2. Marriage is seen as a unbreakable covenant.
3. Each partner is committed to the growth of the other.
4. Sexual and emotional fidelity are maintained.
5. The couple combat boredom by striving not to take one another for granted.

Here are a few rules that have been found to be true about love and marriage.

If you don't respect your partner,
you're going to have a lot of trouble.
If you don't know how to compromise,
you're going to have a lot of trouble.
If you can't talk openly
about what goes on between you,
you're going to have a lot of trouble.
And if you don't have a common set of values in life,
you're going to have a lot of trouble.
To put it positively:
Respect one another.
Be willing to compromise.
Talk openly and truthfully
about what is going on between you.
And strive to have an agreed set of values.

6

Promises to keep

Promises to keep
Who is going to be in control?

Introduction

In the name of the Father and of the Son and of the Holy Spirit.

The grace of our Lord Jesus Christ, the love of God, and the fellowship of the Holy Spirit be with you all.

Today N. and N. are making a solemn promise to one another. They are promising to be faithful to one another in love for the rest of their lives. This is the most important promise they will ever make. We are happy to join them in celebrating this great event in their lives.

Wedding Ceremony without Mass

They are making their promises before God, thereby acknowledging their need of God's help. Let us turn to God now, and ask his blessing on them, and on all gathered here. [Pause]

Opening Prayer

God of power and love, look with kindness on N. and N. who today are being united in the sacrament of marriage. In your goodness, save them from the darkness of broken promises, and help them to walk in the light of faithful love. We ask this through Christ our Lord.

Wedding Ceremony within Mass

Penitential Rite

All of us have made promises of one kind or another. Let us reflect for a moment on the fact that while it is easy to make a promise, it is not always easy to carry it out. [Pause]

Let us ask forgiveness for our infidelities, and the strength to be faithful in the future.

I confess to almighty God ...

May almighty God have mercy on us, forgive us our sins, and bring us to everlasting life.

Opening Prayer
As above

Suggested Reading
C5, p. 135.

Homily

Promises figure very prominently in the Bible. There we see how God's people are constantly led forward by promises. And promises figure prominently in our lives too.

47

The great thing about a promise is that it gives us a goal to aim at. People who have no goal are aimless, and tend to stagnate. A promise motivates and energises us. A promise has to be worked for. It forces us to struggle for something, and this is a good thing.

Vows or promises of their nature reach out to an unknown future. On the day we make a promise, we have no idea where it will lead us or what it will demand of us. It is only after we begin to deliver on the promise that these things are gradually revealed to us.

Another thing: on the day we make a promise we may know very little about ourselves. We may think that we are strong, brave and generous. The fact that the going may be easy at the beginning serves to reinforce our belief in our own virtue. But as the years go by, and the promise begins to make demands on us, we learn a painful and humbling truth about ourselves. We learn that we are self-divided; that we are a mixture of strength and weakness, courage and cowardice, generosity and selfishness. We can never know how we will act under new circumstances. It's easy to renege in difficult times on what we promised in rosier times.

A promise reveals a lot about the character of the one who makes it. People are all alike in the making of promises. It is in the carrying out of promises that they differ. The promises of some dissolve like salt in water.

So what shall we do? Venture nothing? No. We have to know what we are doing, and see the goal we are aiming at as worth-while. And we have to know that there is a price to be paid. A promise calls for trust, commitment, and willingness to sacrifice oneself. And every promise has to be remade many times.

N. and N. are about to exchange their marriage vows. They are promising lasting fidelity to one another. The marriage promise is something enormous. It means choosing one direction and closing off all others.

The fact that a (young) couple are prepared to embrace that kind of commitment is a sign of hope for the world. All the more so when we realise what a short distance they can see ahead, and the fact that they are not even aware of their own deficiencies.

Faithfulness is one of the greatest and most necessary things in life. But it is not easy. If one wishes to be faithful, one must be prepared to put oneself, one's pleasures, comforts, and interests in second place.

Faithfulness is the ability to stick with one's choice. Even though it is not easy, it brings great rewards. There is no happiness or growth except in the fulfilment of one's obligations. If N. and N. are faithful to their promises, they can expect the greatest measure of happiness a man and woman can have.

God knows what we are made of. N. and N. are making their promises before God. In so doing they are saying, 'Lord, help us to be faithful.' Through the sacrament of marriage God's grace will be available to them. The Lord's support and strength is tendered daily to a couple striving, against obstacles, to give witness to the power of lasting love.

Prayer of the Faithful

President   God is the source of all life. Let us now pray earnestly to God for the strength to persevere on the difficult but rewarding path of faithfulness.

Response   Lord, hear our prayer.

Reader(s)   For Christians: that they may never allow words to take the place of deeds. [Pause] Let us pray to the Lord.

For those who hold public office: that their deeds may match their words and promises. [Pause] Let us pray to the Lord.

For N. and N.: that God may grant them the graces necessary to fulfil the promises they have made to each other. [Pause] Let us pray to the Lord.

For all here present: that God may bless us with a generous and faithful love so that we may be true to our promises. [Pause] Let us pray to the Lord.

For the victims of broken promises: that they may find healing and peace. [Pause] Let us pray to the Lord.

For those who have died, especially ...(here we could mention anyone who was related to the bride or groom): that God may fulfil for them his promise of eternal life. [Pause] Let us pray to the Lord.

President Lord our God, you are always faithful to your promises. Look with kindness on us in our weakness. Grant
that what we have said with our lips, we may believe
with our hearts, and practise with our lives. We make
this prayer through Christ our Lord.

Blessing

May God save you from the darkness of broken promises.
May God enable you to walk in the light of faithful love.
May you know that, no matter what, God will always be faithful
to you.

Reflection – PROMISES TO KEEP

At the core of marriage are the promises the partners make to one
another. But, as we all know from experience, promises are easy to
make but not always easy to keep.

In his poem, *Stopping By Woods On A Snowy Evening,* Robert
Frost shows how easily we can be side-tracked, and consequently
how important it is to keep reminding ourselves of our promises.

Whose woods these are I think I know,
His house is in the village though;
He will not see me stopping here
To watch his woods fill up with snow.

My little horse must think it queer
To stop without a farm house near;
Between the woods and frozen lake
The darkest evening of the year.

He gives his harness bells a shake
To ask if there is some mistake;
The only other sound is the sweep
Of easy wind and downy flake.

The woods are lovely, dark and deep;
But I have promises to keep,
And miles to go before I sleep,
And miles to be before I sleep.

Reflection – WHO IS GOING TO BE IN CONTROL?

The issue as to who is going to be in control
is a major issue in any relationship.
To control others is to have power over them
so that we can force them to do our will
whether they want to or not.
Those who wield power over others oppress them,
trying to turn them into slaves or copies of themselves.
Power offers an easy substitute for the hard task of love.
It's easier to control people that to love people.
Power and love are incompatible.
Each partner must give up the desire to control the other.
Giving up control is often seen as weakness
whereas it is strength.
The strong, self-confident person
doesn't need to win every battle
and to be always in control.
If you want to love and be loved,
give up control.

7
Building a relationship

A relationship needs to be nurtured
The dimensions of marriage

Introduction

In the name of the Father and of the Son and of the Holy Spirit.

The grace of our Lord Jesus Christ, the love of God, and the fellowship of the Holy Spirit be with you all.

As human beings we need close ties with other human beings. Without such ties we would be a prey to anguish and loneliness. For our mental health, each of us needs a friend.

N. and N. have developed a close friendship with one another. Today they are committing themselves to one another in marriage, and thus cementing their friendship. We are happy for them, and pray that they will find warmth and closeness in their marriage.

Wedding Ceremony without Mass

Though we long for closeness we also fear it, because it makes demands on us. Let us ask God for the help we need in order to live up to the demands of friendship. [Pause]

Opening Prayer

God, our Father, your love for us is everlasting. Bless N. and N., who today are being united in marriage. Bind them to one another in a relationship of love and trust. May they find in this relationship the warmth and tenderness we all need and long for. We ask this through Christ our Lord.

Wedding within Mass

Penitential Rite

Though we long for closeness we also fear it, because it makes demands on us. Let us turn to God, and ask for his forgiveness and help. [Pause]

Lord Jesus, you reveal to us the mystery of the Father's unconditional love for us. Lord, have mercy.

You remind us of our dignity as God's precious daughters and sons, and help us to live up to that dignity. Christ, have mercy.

You are with us when we walk through the valley of darkness to give us courage and hope. Lord, have mercy

May almighty God have mercy on us, forgive us our sins, and bring us to everlasting life.

Opening Prayer
As above

Suggested Reading
A4, p. 125.

Homily

In his delightful little book, *The Little Prince*, Antoine de Saint Exupery tells the story of a small boy who came to earth from another planet. On earth he felt very lonely and longed for a friend. One day he met a fox who was as desperate for friendship as he was. He asked the fox to play with him.

'I can't because no one has taken the trouble to tame me,' the fox answered.

'What does "to tame" mean?' asked the Little Prince

'It means to establish ties,' the fox replied.

'And what does "to establish ties" mean?' the Little Prince persisted.

'Just that,' said the fox. 'To me you are still nothing more than a little boy like a thousand other little boys. And to you I am nothing more than a fox like a thousand other foxes. But if you tame me, then to me you will be unique in all the world. And to you I will be unique in all the world.'

'I'm beginning to understand,' said the Little Prince.

'If you want a friend, tame me,' said the fox.

'What must I do to tame you?' asked the Little Prince.

'You must be very patient,' replied the fox. 'First you will sit down a little distance from me in the grass. I will look at you out of the corner of my eye, and you will say nothing. Words are a source of misunderstanding. Every day you will sit a little closer to me.'

The Little Prince agreed to tame the fox, and in time they became the best of friends.

We all need friendship. However, friendship doesn't come without cost. Friendship is not just a nice feeling among people who get along well together, but something which calls for a willingness to make sacrifices and undergo pain for another.

Wherever you find a good marriage you will find a deep relationship. Such a relationship does not just happen. It has to be built. The building of it takes time and effort. You can't plant an acorn today and expect to sit in the shade of an oak tree tomorrow.

Both partners have to contribute to the building of the relationship. Since this relationship will profoundly influence their lives, they must be determined to put their marriage above everything else.

They must not be surprised if they experience difficulties. Gold fish in a bowl seem to get along easily. But bring two human beings together and you soon have problems. When two people get married they bring to it, not only their strengths, but also their weaknesses. Therefore difficulties and conflicts are bound to arise. They should not be too proud to seek help if they feel they need it. Difficulties can become opportunities for growth. There is more depth to a relationship that has weathered some storms.

In building a relationship small things are very important. A grand gesture now and then is not enough. The partners must try to achieve intimacy in the little things of every day. They must take an interest in one another. They must pay attention to one another. Listening is the most important form of attention. They must affirm one another. They must be thankful for the gifts and difference of personality in each other. Differences enrich a relationship.

One of the most necessary things in any relationship is trust. Trust is the thing that holds the relationship together through the inevitable trials and tribulations. Trust is built on discipline, reliability, and constancy. When trust is betrayed great hurt results, and the relationship begins to crumble.

Another thing: each must give up the desire to control the other. Giving up control is often confused with weakness. The strong person doesn't need to win every battle and to always be in control. If you want to love and be loved, give up control.

In our times many of the traditional external supports of marriage have gone. Today the partners have to fall back on their own innate strengths, and their own capacity for faithfulness. And today couples have to struggle to balance work and family.

We pray that N. and N. will take the time and make the effort to build a really good relationship in which they will find closeness and love. May they truly tame one another and, like the fox and the Little Prince, become the best of friends.

Prayer of the Faithful

President   It was not we who first loved God. It was God who first
loved us. Let us ask God to touch our hearts, and make
us people who are capable of true love.

Response   Lord, hear our prayer.

Reader(s)   For the Church: that it may be a true community, where people can find warmth and support in the journey of faith. [Pause] Let us pray to the Lord.

For those who hold public office: that their deeds may match their words and promises. [Pause] Let us pray to the Lord.

For N. and N.: that they may build a relationship in which they will find that intimacy we all need and long for. [Pause] Let us pray to the Lord.

That they may find comfort in time of sorrow, strength in time of trial, and be blessed with an enduring love for one another. [Pause] Let us pray to the Lord.

For all married couples: that the partners may strive to be true and loyal friends to one another. [Pause] Let us pray to the Lord.

For all those who are lonely, and who long for love and friendship. [Pause] Let us pray to the Lord.

For those who have died, especially ...(here we could mention anyone who was related to the bride or groom): that freed from every shadow of death, they may take their place in the new creation where all tears are wiped away. [Pause] Let us pray to the Lord.

President: Merciful God, help us to be conscious of the fact that we have the power to bring happiness or misery to those with whom we live; and realising this, may we strive always to treat them the way we would like them to treat us. We ask this through Christ our Lord.

Blessing

May the Lord guide you in the way of love.
May the Lord surround you with his favour as with a shield.
May the Lord bless your home with the laughter of children.

Reflection – A RELATIONSHIP NEEDS TO BE NURTURED

Wherever you find a good marriage
you will find a deep relationship.
Such a relationship does not just happen.
It has to be built.
Both partners have to play their part.
The building of it takes time and effort.
If you want a fruit tree to prosper
you can't just plant it and then forget about it.
You have to nurture it.
In the same way a relationship needs to be nurtured.
How do we nurture a relationship?
A relationship is sustain and nurtured
by the practice of virtues such as
kindness, gentleness, patience, and mutual forgiveness.
Small things are very important.
The partners must try to achieve intimacy
in the little things of every day.
They must take an interest in one another.
They must pay attention to one another.
They must affirm one another.
They must be thankful for the gifts
and difference of personality in each other.
Differences enrich a relationship.
The partners must guard against
taking each other for granted.
They have to put their marriage above everything else.

Reflection – THE DIMENSIONS OF MARRIAGE

There are three dimensions to marriage:
outer, inner, and secret.
The *outer dimension* is its socially recognised form:
man and woman joining together in a lifelong partnership.
It includes the making of a home and a family.
Important though this outer dimension is,
by itself it is no longer enough to bind two people together.

What is more crucial today is the *inner dimension*.
The inner dimension consists of the nature and quality
of a couple's interaction with one another.
Finally, there is the *secret dimension* of marriage.
This is the inner transformation that occurs as a result
of two people's interaction with one another.
This inner dimension tends to mirror
what is happening in the external relationship.
All three dimensions mutually enhance one another.
If any of them are missing,
a couple's life together will be that much poorer.
Some couples may have a strong inner connection,
but seem to be unable to create a healthy,
vibrant lifestyle on the outer plane.
Other couples may make a beautiful home together,
but their exchanges with each other remain shallow.
When a couple can create a world together,
relate deeply to each other,
and continually refine their natures through their interaction,
their life together will be fertile and creative.

8
It's not good to be alone

Spaces in your togetherness
Encountering the other

Introduction

In the name of the Father and of the Son and of the Holy Spirit.

The grace of our Lord Jesus Christ, the love of God, and the fellowship of the Holy Spirit be with you all.

No human being is an island, complete in itself. Each of us is part of the continent of humanity. Hence, we need the company, support, and love of other human beings. Here marriage can play a vital role. Through marriage a man and a woman can achieve that closeness we all need and long for.

We are gathered to witness N. and N. commit themselves to one another in the sacrament of marriage. We are in the presence of love, for it is love that has motivated them to undertake this commitment. This means we are also in the presence of God, for where love is, God is.

Wedding Ceremony without Mass

Let us reflect for a moment on God's love for us, and ask his blessing on N. and N., and on all gathered here. [Pause]
Opening Prayer
Almighty and ever-loving God, when you created humankind you willed that man and wife should be one. Bind N. and N. in the loving union of marriage, so that they may be witnesses to your divine love in the world. We ask this through Christ our Lord.

Wedding within Mass

Penitential Rite

God wants us to be loving towards, and supportive of, one another. Let us reflect on this for a moment. [Pause]

God sets the example himself in his dealings with us.

Lord, you are faithful in all your words and loving in all your deeds. Lord, have mercy.

You support all who fall, and raise up all who are bowed down. Christ, have mercy.

You are close to all who call on you, who call on you from their hearts. Lord, have mercy.

May almighty God have mercy on us, forgive us our sins, and bring us to everlasting life.

Opening Prayer
As above

Suggested Reading

A2, p. 124.

Homily

A tree planted in an exposed place is at the mercy of every wind that blows. This makes it very vulnerable. If it survives at all, it will be in a stunted form. If you want a tree to grow to its full potential, you must plant it in a more sheltered place. And ideally you should plant some other trees near it. For the best results, the trees should be more or less equal.

It is of vital importance to get the space between the trees right. They must be close enough to be able to provide shelter and protection for one another. But they must not be so close that they smother one another. Each tree must have room to grow to its full potential.

It is not good for a tree to be alone. And the Bible says, it is not good for a human being to be alone. We need other people in order to become all that God intended us to become. To feel this need is not a sign of sickness but of health. Without a close relationship with at least one other human being we will be at the mercy of the cold winds of loneliness.

God first gave Adam the animals. But Adam was unable to find a suitable partner among them. Then God gave Adam a woman, Eve. And Adam recognised in her a fitting companion and partner. She was made of the same material as himself, possessed the same dignity as himself, and therefore was his equal. True community can be created only among equals. And so, leaving his parents, Adam joined himself to Eve, and they became 'one body'.

This doesn't mean that they became completely one. This is neither possible nor desirable. When two people get married they become like those trees we talked about earlier. In the ideal marriage there is both closeness and space. The closeness means the partners are able to provide mutual support for one another. The space ensures that they do not stifle one another's growth.

How to achieve closeness without stifling or dominating one another is a great challenge. It calls for a special kind of love. False love seeks to keep the other in subjection. It dreads the idea that the

61

other should have a separate life, with separate interests, separate friends, and separate goals. True love, on the other hand, respects the right, indeed the need, of the other to be an autonomous person.

The couple must be united in such a way that their separateness and loneliness are overcome, yet they are free to be themselves. Their differences are not denied, much less suppressed. Rather, they are encouraged, and so become a source of mutual enrichment.

Today N. and N. are committing themselves to one another in marriage. They are in effect saying to each other: 'I'm ready to stand by your side. I'll be there with you, yet I have no desire to smother, or dominate, or possess you. I'll be there to help you to grow to your full potential. I hope that you can do the same for me.'

Trees cannot receive everything they need from one another. They must also receive from outside sources — from the sun, the rain, the soil ... In the same way a couple cannot give to one another all that they need. They must be open to receive from outside sources — from other people and, above all, from God. We are not trees. We are God's precious children. God wants to see us grow and have life.

Every marriage is bound to know difficulties. But this is not necessarily a bad thing. Trees that grow on hard ground have firmer roots, and thus are better equipped to meet the inevitable storms. In the same way, there is more depth to a relationship that has weathered some storms.

Prayer of the Faithful

President Let us pray to God that he may take away our hearts of stone and give us hearts that are capable of true love.

Response Lord, hear us in your love.

Reader(s) For the Christian community: that its members may love one another as Christ wished. [Pause] Let us pray in faith.

For the heads of governments: that through goodwill and cooperation they may free the world of poverty and oppression, so that all of God's children may live in freedom and dignity. [Pause] Let us pray in faith.

For N and N.: that their relationship may provide them with mutual love and support, without in any way hindering their individual growth and development. [Pause] Let us pray in faith.

That they may find comfort in time of sorrow, strength in time of trial, and be blessed with an enduring love for one another. [Pause] We pray in faith.

For those who are sick, or lonely, or discouraged: that they may find strength through faith in God and the support of the Christian community. [Pause] Let us pray in faith.

For those who have died, especially ... (here we could mention anyone who was related to the bride or groom): that God may give them a seat at the banquet of eternal life. [Pause]

President   God of mercy, fill our hearts with your love. Give us the grace to rise above our human weakness, and keep us faithful to you and to one another. We ask this through Christ our Lord.

Blessing

May you know the joy that springs up in the hearts of those who say 'yes' to love.

May you know the sweetness that falls like dew into the hearts of those who treat others kindly.

And may the Lord bless your home with the laughter of children.

Reflection – SPACES IN YOUR TOGETHERNESS

Marriage implies the coming together of two people. But this doesn't mean that the two become completely one. This is neither possible nor desirable. In the ideal marriage there is both closeness and space. The closeness means the partners are able to provide mutual support for one another. The space ensures that they do not stifle one another's growth.

How to achieve closeness without stifling or dominating one

another is a great challenge. It calls for a special kind of love. False love seeks to keep the other in subjection. True love respects the right, and need, of the other to be an autonomous person.

The couple must be united in such a way that their separateness and loneliness are overcome, yet they are free to be themselves. Their differences are encouraged, and so become a source of mutual enrichment. This is the only foundation on which a mature marriage can be based and real love can grow.

All of this has been put beautifully by Kahlil Gibran.

You are together now,
and together you shall be for ever more,
But let there be spaces in your togetherness,
and let the winds of heaven dance between you.
Love one another, but make not a bond of love:
let it rather be a moving sea
between the shores of your souls.
Fill each other's cup
but drink not from the same cup.
Give one another of your bread
but eat not from the same loaf.
Sing and dance together and be joyous,
but let each one of you be alone,
even as the strings of a lute are alone
though they quiver with the same music.
Give your hearts,
but not into each other's keeping.
For only the hand of Life can contain your hearts.
And stand together yet not too near together;
for the pillars of the temple stand apart,
and the oak tree and the cypress
grow not in each other's shadow.

Reflection – ENCOUNTERING THE OTHER

During the course of our lives we have lots of meetings with people. Most of these turn out to be of little significance, and are soon forgotten. You could meet some people every day, but it's like a meeting between strangers. You never get close to them. This is one of the great sadnesses of life.

But other meetings turn out to be of great significance. They enrich our lives and sometimes change them utterly. You may have just one meeting with someone, and an immediate bond is formed. This is one of the most delightful and rewarding experiences in life.

A husband and wife can be together
and yet never really encounter one another.
They can live in the same house,
sleep in the same bed,
eat at the same table,
kneel in the same church pew,
exchange many words,
and yet never really meet.
Though living side by side,
they remain separate, lonely creatures,
like shells on a shore.
But they can encounter one another.
In an encounter, all barriers fall down,
and all pretence is set aside;
they open their hearts to one another,
so that life flows from one to the other.
An encounter is a strange and wonderful thing.
When it happens, people are transformed.

9
The bond of love

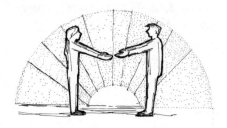

The bond of marriage
Levels of connection

Introduction

In the name of the Father and of the Son and of the Holy Spirit.

The grace of our Lord Jesus Christ, the love of God, and the fellowship of the Holy Spirit be with you all.

Today is a day of destiny for N. and N. After today their destinies will be inextricably bound up with one another. During this ceremony they will bind themselves to one another by a very special bond – the bond of marriage. God blesses this bond and wishes it to endure.

Wedding Ceremony without Mass

Unfortunately, because of our human weakness, we don't find it easy to be faithful to our commitments. We need God to help us. Let us turn to God now, and invoke his blessing on N. and N., and on all gathered here. [Pause]

Opening Prayer

Almighty and ever-living God, when you created humankind you willed that husband and wife should be one. Bind N. and N. in the loving union of marriage. Make their love fruitful so that they may be living witnesses to your divine love in the world. We ask this through Christ our Lord.

Wedding within Mass

Penitential Rite

It is fitting that this ceremony is taking place in the context of the Eucharist. The Eucharist creates a bond between the disciples of Christ, a bond which he wishes to endure. Let us call to mind our sins which weaken our ties with Christ and with one another. [Pause]

We need the Lord's help. Let us turn to the Lord now and ask for that help.

Lord, you are the vine, we are the branches. Lord, have mercy.

Separated from you and from one another, our lives become barren. Christ, have mercy.

United with you and with one another, our lives become fruitful. Lord, have mercy.

May almighty God have mercy on us, forgive us our sins, and bring us to everlasting life.

Opening Prayer
As above

Suggested Reading

A1, p. 123, or A2, p. 124.

Homily

When two people get married we talk about them 'tying the knot'. Thus we acknowledge that a bond is formed between them. From this day forward their lives are linked together. They are committed to one another. They are responsible to and for one another. They are bound together in a relationship that will profoundly influence their lives.

They lose something. There is a certain loss of autonomy and independence. The marriage commitment imposes certain constraints. It requires sacrifices. The partners cannot be as free and independent as they were when they were single.

But they stand to gain a lot more. The bond is not a fetter which makes one or both of them prisoners. Rather, it is a lifeline which provides them with some very precious things, such as companionship, friendship, and mutual support.

To link one's entire future to that of another person is an enormous thing to do. It involves a 'leap of faith'. Hence it is not something to be undertaken lightly. The partners must know what they are doing and also know each other. And it must be done in complete freedom. It is not the Church or the State but *they* who are tying the knot. They are not being driven into this union. They are being drawn into it by their love for one another. Without love the bond of marriage would become a fetter.

Today N. and N. are joining their lives in this public ceremony. We are talking about the union of two personalities, of two minds, and two hearts. The bond by which they are linking their lives together is not made of unbreakable material. It is made of human and therefore imperfect material. And we can be sure that it will be tested. In what ways we don't know, and wouldn't like to speculate. But one thing we can be sure of: it will be subjected to the normal wear and tear, stresses and strains, of human relationships.

What is it that would weaken this bond?

Breaches of trust, lack of communication, and selfishness. When selfishness is present love dies. Besides, to seek only one's own happiness is the surest way to remain unhappy.

All of these gnaw away at the bond. But there is one thing that is especially destructive of a relationship. That is infidelity.

On top of these there are the corrosive cultural influences that can make divorce seem almost inevitable. Since the traditional external supports have gone, the couple have to fall back on their own innate strengths, and their own capacity for faithfulness.

What is that will strengthen the bond?

Trust – this is a core value. Trust is the thing that holds the relationship together through the inevitable trials and tribulations.

Good communication. This is probably the most important ingredient is the everyday health of a relationship. It enables couples to solve problems together. It involves not just speaking but also listening. Without communication there can be no unity of heart.

Unselfishness.

And fidelity. Not just physical fidelity, which is already a great thing, but fidelity of the heart. Fidelity of the heart means that my partner has a special place in my heart which no one else will ever have.

N. and N., the future, with its successes and failures, its joys and its sorrows, is hidden from your eyes. Even so, you are prepared to take each other for better or for worse, for richer or for poorer, in sickness and in health, until death.

God blesses the bond which you are forming with one another today, and pledges you the life-long support of his grace in the sacrament of marriage. The fragility of the bond should make you eager to seek God's help. Marriage is a sacrament of love, which draws its strength from God, who is the source of love.

Prayer of the Faithful

President   In and through his Son, God has bound himself to us by a bond that can never be broken. Let us ask God to strengthen the bonds that bind us to one another.

Response   Lord, hear us in your love.

Reader(s)   For the Christian community: that it may be a sign of unity in a divided world. [Pause] We pray in faith.

For world leaders: that they may take the path of reconciliation and peace rather than that of conflict and war. [Pause] We pray in faith.

For N. and N.: that the frail human bond by which they join their lives today may prove to be an unbreakable bond of love. [Pause] We pray in faith.

That this bond may bind them together in a union, not only of body, but also of mind and heart. [Pause] We pray in faith.

For all married couples: that they may keep in mind the love which brought them together in the first place, and so continue to offer one another companionship and support. [Pause] We pray in faith.

For marriages that have broken down: that God may grant them healing and peace. [Pause] We pray in faith.

For single and widowed people: that they may find love and support in the Christian community. [Pause] We pray in faith.

For those who have died, especially … (here we could mention anyone who was related to the bride or groom): that God may bring them into the light of his presence. [Pause] We pray in faith.

President   Merciful God, fill our hearts with your love. Give us the grace to rise above our human weakness, and keep us faithful to you and to one another. We ask this through Christ our Lord.

Blessing

May God, the almighty Father, bless you with joy.

May the only Son of God have mercy on you, and help you in good times and in bad.

May the Holy Spirit of God fill your hearts with his love.

Reflection – THE BOND OF MARRIAGE

When two people get married
their fates becomes inextricably intertwined.
They become like two climbers on the one rope.
If they pull together,
they have an excellent chance of making it to the top.
But if they pull against one another,
they risk falling into the abyss.
The bond is not meant to be a fetter,
making one or both of them prisoners.
It is meant to be a lifeline
which provides them with companionship,
friendship, and mutual support.
The bond is not made of unbreakable material,
and we can be sure that it will be tested by life.
What is it that weakens this bond?
Breaches of trust,
lack of communication,
selfishness,
and infidelity.
And what is it that strengthens the bond?
The opposite of the these:
trust,
good communication,
unselfishness,
and fidelity.
Not just physical fidelity, but fidelity of the heart.
Fidelity of the heart means
that my partner has a special place in my heart
which no one else will ever have.

Reflection – LEVELS OF CONNECTION

In any intimate relationship
there can be a number of levels of connection.
The first level is the desire for *companionship:*
just being together, sharing interests and activities.
A further level happens when two people share

common interests, goals, and values.
They create a shared world;
they from a *community*.
Beyond sharing values and interests
lies *communication*.
On this level they share what is going on inside them:
their thoughts, feelings, hopes, and dreams.
A further extension of communication is *communion*.
This goes beyond sharing thoughts and feelings.
It involves a deep recognition of the other person's being.
This often takes place in silence,
and consists in just being together.

10

When two roads meet

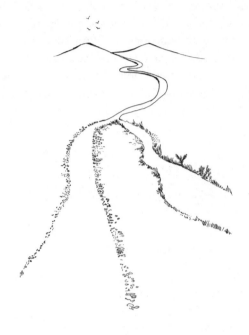

Slow down
Crossing over

Introduction

In the name of the Father and of the Son and of the Holy Spirit.

The grace of our Lord Jesus Christ, the love of God, and the fellowship of the Holy Spirit be with you all.

Married or single, all of us are embarked on a great journey – the journey of life. To know that others are on the same road as ourselves is a great comfort. But to have them as companions is better still.

For several years N. and N. had been making their separate ways along the path of life. But at a certain point their paths met and they became friends. Today they make the decision to travel the rest of life's journey together. This is truly a day of destiny for them.

We are gathered here to witness as they commit themselves to one another and to their common journey. We are in the presence of love, for only love could motivate people to take a step like this. This means we are also in the presence of God, for where love is, God is.

Wedding Ceremony without Mass

Therefore let us draw near to God, and ask his blessing on N. and N., and on all gathered here. [Pause]

Opening Prayer

God of love and mercy, hear our prayers for N. and N., who today are committing themselves to one another, and setting out on the road of married life. Send your blessing upon them. Grant that the lamp of love may always light their way, so that they may follow their chosen road in peace and joy. We ask this through Christ our Lord.

Wedding within Mass

Penitential Rite

Let us draw near to God who is with us now and at every step of life's journey. [Pause]

Let us ask God's forgiveness for our sins and failings.

I confess to almighty God …

May almighty God have mercy on us, forgive us our sins, and bring us to everlasting life.

Opening Prayer
As above

Suggested Reading
A7, p. 127.

Homily

Marriage implies the coming together of two people and two lives. This coming together must be not only one of bodies but also one of minds and hearts. 'Physical relationship divorced from spiritual is body without soul' (Gandhi).

But this doesn't mean that the two become completely one. They are not like two streams which converge and then coalesce. The partners keep their individual identities, and that is a good thing.

A better image is that of two travellers, travelling on different paths, who meet and decide to travel together from that point on. We are not talking about two strangers who meet when out for an afternoon stroll, and who decide to finish their stroll together but then go their separate ways. We are talking about a man and woman, on the great and unretraceable path of life, who meet and make the momentous decision to travel together for the rest of their lives.

Each says to the other: 'Will you walk the rest of life's road with me? Are you willing to share your life with me as I am with you?' To give an unqualified 'yes' to these questions is a huge undertaking. To commit one's hopes and dreams, one's entire life and destiny, to another human being is an enormous thing to do.

When two people come together in this way there is a certain loss. For instance, there is a loss of independence. Each can no longer 'go it alone'. But there is a far greater gain. A great sharing takes place. A great mutual enrichment results.

For a start, they now have companionship. How sweetly and swiftly the milestones go by when we have pleasant company. They also have mutual support and encouragement so that they are able to take the difficulties in their stride. But above all they have that magical thing called 'love', without which all of us are forlorn travellers on this earth. When friendly paths meet, the whole world becomes like home.

It is interesting to consider how the paths of partners meet. Sometimes the meeting seems completely accidental. Other times it seems as if a friendly hand steered them gently towards one another.

Sometimes the decision to travel together is taken quickly. Their paths cross once and that is all it takes. In other cases the decision comes only after their paths have crossed and recrossed many times.

No matter the circumstances in which their paths meet, the person with faith is able to say: 'Here is a companion whom God has given me, a companion with whom I can share the rest of my journey.'

Well, N. and N. met, and have decided to travel the rest of the way together. We are here to witness them commit themselves to one another and to their common journey.

The marriage journey is a journey of love. To embark on a journey of love is to embark on a sacred path. But it's not an easy path. Every marriage demands effort and sacrifice to keep it on the right track.

God made us for love – to give it and to receive it. However, the ability to love is not something that is given to the couple on their wedding day with all the other gifts. Love is something that has to be learned. And it is not just for serene days but also for rough and hard days.

We pray that God will help N. and N. to make the journey from selfishness to true love. Whether married or single, this is a journey all of us need to make. For Christians, this is the real journey of life.

The road stretches ahead of them. It is a road with many twists and turns. Every turn of the road hides uncertainty but also holds out the possibility of exciting discovery. We pray that God will bless and guide them in their journey.

As they set out into the future together, they might make their own the beautiful words of the French writer, Albert Camus: 'Don't walk ahead of me, I may not follow; don't walk behind me, I may not lead; just walk beside me and be my friend.

Prayer of the Faithful

President: Though we may be travelling along separate paths, we are all travelling towards God's Kingdom. Let us pray to God for the grace to be helpful to one another.

Response Lord, hear our prayer.

Reader(s) For all those who believe in Christ: that they may remember his commandment: love one another as I have loved you. [Pause] Let us pray to the Lord.

For those who hold public office: that they may judge wisely and act justly. [Pause] Let us pray to the Lord.

For N. and N.: that their path may be lit up by the lamp of a true and faithful love for one another. [Pause] Let us pray to the Lord.

That God, who brought them to this day, may establish their marriage in love and preserve it in peace. [Pause] Let us pray to the Lord.

For all married couples: that they may keep in mind the love which brought them together in the first place, and so continue to offer one another companionship and support. [Pause] Let us pray to the Lord.

For those who travel the road of life alone: that they may find companionship in the Christian community. [Pause] Let us pray to the Lord.

For those who have died, especially ... (here we could mention anyone who was related to the bride or groom): that God may bring them to the promised land of eternal life. [Pause]

President: All-powerful God, grant us in all our tasks your help, in all our doubts your guidance, in all our weaknesses your strength, in all our sorrows your consolation, and in all our dangers your protection. We ask this through Christ our Lord.

Blessing

N. & N., you are setting out today on the road of married life.

May the road rise to meet you, and may the wind of God's grace be behind you.

May the sun of God's love shine warmly on you, and the rain of God's mercy fall softly on you.

And may the God of love, who brought you together, hold you both in the hollow of his hand.

Reflection – CROSSING OVER

When two people get married they leave one world and enter another. They give up the single way of life and all it entails in the hope of gaining a life of love and union. However, they cannot gain the good things of the new world unless they let go of those of the old world.

For this reason, getting married could be compared to crossing a bridge, a bridge with a difference. Once you cross this bridge you can't return. Therefore, you can't walk casually across. You have to think carefully about what you are doing.

The first thing you do is look back. You think about the things you are leaving behind. Now that you are about to say good-bye to them, they assume an exaggerated importance. We are not talking merely about material things.

Then you look ahead, and think of what you are hoping to find on the other side. Without doubt, at least from here, they appear very attractive. Still, they are not yet yours. For a while at least, you will have to live on hope, which means risk and uncertainty.

So far you have been thinking only of what you are leaving behind and what you are hoping to find up ahead. But now you begin to think of the most important thing of all, namely, what you are taking with you. Once again we are not talking about material things, but about something infinitely more valuable. We are talking about the kind of person you are, or what you have made of yourself. This is the only thing that is truly yours. No one can take it from you, though you can agree to share it.

It is a mighty step that you are taking. But what makes it easy and joyful is the fact that you are not making it alone. You have a partner by your side who is taking the same step because of a commitment to you.

So, you join hands, and walk into the future together. The prayers and good wishes of your friends put wind in your sails.

Reflection – SLOW DOWN

Though the stream was in a hurry to reach the plains,
nevertheless, it took time to form pools.
Around these pools grass grew,
from them animals quenched their thirst,
and within them frogs jumped for joy.
Today people are always rushing.
They seem unable to slow down
and spend time with one another.
No wonder they offer one another so little.
It's hard to drink from a fast-flowing stream.
Friendship is about having time for someone,
spending time with that person,
being present to that person,
so that life can flow from one to the other.
The greatest gift I can give to another person
is the gift of my time.
To give of my time is to give of myself.
If I wish to nourish another person
I must allow the stream of my life
to slow down and form a pool.
From that pool the other will drink.

I I
Building on rock

Love is not a readymade garment
Presence and absence

Introduction

In the name of the Father and of the Son and of the Holy Spirit.

The grace of our Lord Jesus Christ, the love of God, and the fellowship of the Holy Spirit be with you all.

Today N. and N. are setting out to build a very important house — the house of their marriage. People enter marriage with great hopes. But many place their hopes on flimsy things and build on weak foundations.

The teaching of Jesus shows us the way to go. To those who listen to his words and act on them, he makes a wonderful promise. He says they are building the house of their lives on solid rock.

Wedding Ceremony without Mass
Let us reflect for a moment on how much we need God's help and guidance. [Pause]

Opening Prayer

Almighty and ever-living God, your love for us is the same yesterday, today, and forever. Bless N. and N., who today are being united in the sacrament of marriage. Help them to build the house of their marriage on the values of the Gospel, and give them the kind of love that will enable them to live in harmony with one another, and in peace with others. We make this prayer through Christ our Lord.

Wedding within Mass

Penitential Rite

Let us pause for a moment to see what place the teachings of Christ and the values of the Gospel have in our lives. [Pause]

Let us now turn to the Lord, confident that he will help and guide us.

Lord Jesus, you help us to place our trust in God rather than in material things. Lord, have mercy.

You help us to realise that it is more blessed to give than to receive. Christ, have mercy.

You help us to realise that to live rightly is what life is about. Lord, have mercy.

May almighty God have mercy on us, forgive us our sins, and bring us to everlasting life.

Opening Prayer
As above

Suggested Reading
E3, p. 139.

Homily

The most important part of a house is largely invisible, so much so that normally we don't even think about it. But a builder does. In fact it the very first thing he thinks about. We're talking about the foundation.

The foundation of a house has to be deep and solid. In a word — rocklike. To put down such a foundation calls for careful planning, and a lot of hard, unspectacular work. Months go by and there is still nothing to be seen above ground. To the uninitiated time is being wasted.

But the wise builder knows differently. He takes his time. He will not be rushed. He is thinking far into the future. In his mind's eye he already sees the completed building. He sees people living in it, people who have invested their 'all' in that house. He sees the house being beaten by rain and lashed by wind. He knows that the fate of the house and its occupants will depend on the soundness of the foundation he is now laying down.

The foolish builder, on the other hand, is in a hurry. He can't be bothered to go down deep, and he is not too concerned about the quality of the materials he uses. He doesn't hesitate to cut corners. He is not looking to the future. He does not allow himself to think about the people who will live in the house, or the storms that will inevitably assail it. His only concern is to get it up as quickly and as cheaply as possible.

Building a marriage could be compared to building a house. Like a house it does not appear overnight. A couple do not take possession of the house of marriage all ready-made on their wedding day. It has to be built. In building it, it is essential that they look to the future because this house has to last, not just for a few years, but for the rest of their lives. And they can be sure that some gales will be let loose upon it. Hence the importance of laying down a good foundation. They have to build, not on sand, but on rock.

What are the 'rocks' on which the house of marriage needs to be built? Here are a few of them.

Fidelity. This is not just another rock. It is a precious stone, a true gem. We're not talking only about physical fidelity, but also fidelity of the heart.

Trust. Without mutual trust the marriage relationship won't even get off the ground. Trust is the most precious thing we can give to another person. Trust is the thing that holds the relationship together through the inevitable trials and tribulations.

Respect. Respect for one another is the bedrock of any relationship.

Gentleness. To many gentleness means weakness. Nothing could be further from the truth. Gentleness is a form of strength. It takes a strong, self-confident person to be gentle. Gentleness is one of the most necessary things, not just in marriage, but in life in general.

Communication. This is probably the most important ingredient of a relationship. It enables couples to solve problems together. Without communication there can be no unity of heart.

Faith in God. Of ourselves we are very limited. We are weakened by sin and tainted by selfishness. We are incapable of unselfish love and rocklike constancy. Hence we need the help only God can give.

Love. This is the mortar which binds all these stones together. There are many words to express love. This is good, because love takes many forms. However, here we are not talking about words. To build on words, no matter how fine they might be, is, as Jesus said, to build on sand. We are talking about a love which is expressed in deeds.

These deeds don't have to be big ones. They are more likely to be small ones. But small deeds are very important. They may not look much, but they accumulate to create a friendly atmosphere. Small flowers give off little scent on their own, but put a bunch of them together and they can fill a room with fragrance.

What N. and N. are called to build is not a building of stones and mortar, but a small community, one in which they will be able to find acceptance, a sense of belonging, warmth, security and peace. Without these, even though they may be living in a mansion, they won't find in it what they are looking for.

We pray that the house of their marriage will, with the Lord's help, endure. We pray also that they will find in it what their hearts are longing for.

Prayer of the Faithful

President Let us pray for the wisdom, courage, and strength to be able to build our lives, not on the values of the world, but on those of the Gospel.

Response Lord, hear us in your love.

Reader(s) For the followers of Christ: that they may not love merely in word but in deed and in truth. [Pause] We pray in faith.

For our political and civil leaders: that their deeds may match their words. [Pause] We pray in faith.

For N. and N.: that their love for each other may be such that the house of their marriage will stand firm for the whole of their lives. [Pause] We pray in faith.

That, through faith in God and in each other, they may be able to withstand the inevitable storms which will assail this fragile house. [Pause] We pray in faith.

For all here present: that we may derive hope for our lives from this celebration. [Pause] We pray in faith.

For those who have died, especially ...(here we could mention anyone who was related to the bride or groom): that they may dwell in the house of the Lord for ever. [Pause] We pray in faith.

President Almighty and ever-loving God, grant us in all our tasks your help, in all our doubts your guidance, in all our weaknesses your strength, in all our sorrows your consolation, and in all our dangers your protection. We ask this through Christ our Lord.

Blessing

May you be poor in misfortune, and rich in blessings.

May you be slow to make enemies, and quick to make friends.

And may the Lord bless your home with the laughter of children.

Reflection – LOVE IS NOT A READY-MADE GARMENT

Love is not a ready-made garment,
but a piece of material to be cut and tailored.
It is not an apartment ready for occupation,
but a house to be designed, built, furnished and repaired.
It is not a conquered peak,
but a daunting ascent with many obstacles and falls
made in the icy cold or the fierce heat.
It is not a safe anchorage in a harbour of happiness,
but a voyage on the open sea in storm and tempest.
It is not a triumphant 'yes', an affirmation of success,
a magnificent final chord followed by clapping and cheers,
but 'yes' repeated again and again throughout life
accompanied by 'no' repeated as many times, but overcome.
It is not the sudden appearance of a new life,
perfect from the moment of its birth,
but the flowing of a river from its source,
sometimes in flood and sometimes only as a trickle of water,
but always on its way to the infinite sea.

Michel Quoist

Reflection – PRESENCE AND ABSENCE

A couple have to spend time together
for a bond to form between them.
However, physical presence doesn't always produce
the intimacy people long for.
In fact, when people spend all their time together,
real friendship between them becomes difficult.
Presence can blind.
Hence, separation is necessary
if the partners are to achieve a deeper union.
In absence they see each other in a new way.
They are less distracted by each other's idiosyncrasies,
and better able to appreciate each other's true worth.
But there is a danger in separation too.
If they are apart for too long,
and communicate too seldom,

the thread of our friendship
may be stretched to breaking point.
There are too opposites to be avoided:
too much company and too little.
For closeness to grow there must be a continuous interplay
between presence and absence.
Lord, grant that we may not be alone when together.
Help us, rather, to be together when alone.

12

A lasting covenant

Faithfulness
Discovering your own wealth

Introduction

In the name of the Father and of the Son and of the Holy Spirit.

The grace of our Lord Jesus Christ, the love of God, and the fellowship of the Holy Spirit be with you all.

No doubt the past days and weeks have been very busy ones for N. & N., and for all who have help them prepare for this day. But now that the moment has arrived, some quiet and stillness are called for. In this stillness we will hear God's word to us, and the words by which N. and N. will pledge their lives to one another in a covenant of love.

Wedding Ceremony without Mass

God has made a covenant of love with us in Christ, a covenant to which he is faithful forever. Let us now turn to God, calling down his blessing on all gathered here, and especially on N. and N. [Pause]

Opening Prayer

God of love and mercy, hear our prayers for N. and N. Bless the covenant of love they are entering today. Seal the bond of marriage by which they will be no longer two but one in mind and heart. Warm their hearts and strengthen their wills so that they may be capable of true and lasting love. We ask this through Christ our Lord.

Wedding Ceremony with Mass

Penitential Rite

It was God who first made a covenant of love with us. God is always faithful to us. However, we may not have always been faithful to God and to one another. Let us turn to God now, and ask pardon our infidelities, and the help to do better in the future. [Pause]

Lord, you are faithful in all your words and loving in all your deeds. Lord, have mercy.

You support all who fall, and raise up all who are bowed down. Christ, have mercy.

You are close to all who call on you, who call on you from their hearts. Lord, have mercy.

May almighty God have mercy on us, forgive us our sins, and bring us to everlasting life.

Opening Prayer

As above

Suggested Reading

A6, p. 127.

Homily

'Covenant' is not a word we use very often in our everyday language. We are more familiar with the word 'contract'. There is a big difference between a contract and a covenant.

A contract is a strictly business arrangement. It is a narrow legal agreement dictated by mutual interest. A contract falls apart when one or both of the partners fail to fulfil their part of the bargain.

A covenant, on the other hand, is based on love and friendship. It involves a commitment to go beyond the letter of the law, and to sustain the relationship even at times when it seems to go against the interests of one of the parties.

Covenant is a key word in the Bible. It is the word that is most frequently used to described God's relationship with his people.

After the story of creation, the story of God's covenant with Abraham is the key moment in the Old Testament. From that point on the Bible becomes the story of God's relationship with his people. It is summed up in the oft-repeated formula: 'You will be my people, and I will be your God.'

God didn't make a contract with us; God made a covenant with us. God could have gone the way of power. But he didn't. He went the way of love. God wants to be loved by us, not feared. If we obey God because we are afraid of him, then God has our obedience but not our love. In order to love and be loved, God has to give us room to choose. The covenant between God and humanity is an agreement entered into by two free parties.

Even though the people broke God's covenant, God did not abandon them. God's steadfast love for his people enjoined on them a reciprocal obligation to God and to one another.

The Bible often compares the covenant between God and his people to a marriage relationship. It's a good comparison. Even though there is a contractual side to marriage, marriage is not a business arrangement. Marriage is essentially a covenant which the two partners freely make with one another.

Today N. and N. are making a covenant with one another. They are pledging themselves to a code of mutual loyalty and protection. God make the first man a 'helpmate'. And so, leaving his parents, the man joined himself to this helpmate, and they became 'one body'. To be one body is to be covenanted together, each in need of the other, each having a special gift to give the other, so that they complement each other.

This kind of commitment is very demanding of weak human beings. Those who have a sure faith are lucky, because another kind of strength becomes available to them. In and through his Son, God has bound himself to us by a bond that can never be broken. We are not just God's people. We are God's sons and daughters. God is faithful to us because he loves us. Fidelity is rooted in love. Where true love exists, fidelity comes naturally and easily.

In the Gospel Jesus talks about the ideal relationship between man and woman in marriage. In its indissoluble fidelity, it mirrors the covenant between God and his people. Marriage is a sacrament of love, which draws its strength from God, who is the source of love.

God looks with love on N. and N. today as they make this solemn covenant of love with one another. Through the sacrament of matrimony his grace will become available to them. The Lord's support and strength is tendered daily to a couple, striving against obstacles, to love one another faithfully.

Prayer of the Faithful

President   In and through his Son, God has bound himself to us in an everlasting covenant of love. Let us ask God to strengthen the bonds that bind us to him and to one another.

Response   Lord, hear us in your love.

Reader(s)   For the Pope and the bishops: that they may sustain the people of God in faith, hope and love. [Pause] We pray in faith.

For our civil and political leaders: that God may help them to fulfil their responsibilities faithfully. [Pause] We pray in faith.

For N. and N.: that God may confirm, sanctify, and preserve the covenant of love which they are making with one another today. [Pause] We pray in faith.

That they may know God's strength in times of weakness, God's guidance in times of doubt, and God's consolation in times of sorrow. [Pause] We pray in faith.

For those who have died, especially ... (here we could mention anyone who was related to the bride or groom): that God may bring them into the light of his presence. [Pause] We pray in faith.

President: God of love and mercy, give us the grace to rise above our human weaknesses, and keep us faithful to you and to one another. We ask this through Christ our Lord.

Blessing

May the Lord bless you and keep you.
May the Lord let his face shine on you and be gracious to you.
May the Lord look kindly on you and give you peace, now and forever.

Reflection – FAITHFULNESS

Being faithful is not
never losing one's way,
never fighting,
never falling.
It is always getting up and going on again.
It is wanting to follow to the end the route
that you have decided on and mapped out together.
It is trusting each other,
beyond the darkness and shadows.
It is supporting one another,
beyond the falls and bruises.
It is having faith in the total power of God's love,
beyond human love itself.

Faithfulness is very often the faithfulness of Jesus,
who was nailed to the cross,
his body and heart tortured by man's lack of faithfulness,
alone,
abandoned,
betrayed,
but who remained faithful to death,
giving and forgiving,
offering his life for us
and saving love for ever.

Michel Quoist

Reflection – DISCOVERING YOUR OWN WEALTH

Many couples enter marriage with unreasonably high expectations. However, they sometimes dump all their expectations on their partner. They expect the partner to have everything they haven't got. And when that doesn't happen, they are disappointed. The truth is: no human being can provide all the love, security, and nurturance we dream of.

What we need to do is connect with ourselves more deeply, and develop our own strength and confidence, instead of waiting for someone else to bring these qualities into our lives. The qualities we seek in a partner are the qualities we need to develop in ourselves. The greatest good a partner can do for us is not to give us of his/her wealth, but to help us to find own wealth.

I lived on the shady side of the road
and watched my neighbours' gardens across the way
revelling in the sunshine.
I felt I was poor
and from door to door went in my hunger.
The more they gave me from their careless abundance
the more I became aware of my beggar's bowl.
Till one morning I awoke from my sleep
at the sudden opening of my door
and you came and asked for alms.
In despair I broke open the lid of my chest
and was startled into finding my own wealth.

Rabindranath Tagore

I3
United at heart

Springtime in the heart
The wounded heart

Introduction

In the name of the Father and of the Son and of the Holy Spirit.

The grace of our Lord Jesus Christ, the love of God, and the fellowship of the Holy Spirit be with you all.

N. and N. have come here to commit themselves to each other in the sacrament of marriage. The greatest riches a couple can bring to their marriage are the riches of the heart. The heart of one person holds inexhaustible sources of life for the heart of another. But for this to happen the heart must be right.

Alas, the heart is not always right. It is sometimes cold, sometimes hard, sometimes closed, sometimes empty, sometimes wounded, and sometimes broken. We need to heal the wounds of the heart in order to be able to love properly.

Wedding Ceremony without Mass

A person is what the heart is. But only God can make the heart what it is meant to be. Let us turn to God now, asking him to kindle in our hearts the fire of his love. [Pause]

Opening Prayer

God of love and mercy, hear our prayers for N. and N., who today are joining their lives in marriage. May they cast aside all doubts and fears, and open their hearts fully and unreservedly to one another, and thus build a community of love and peace. We ask this through our Lord Jesus Christ, your Son, who lives and reigns with you and the Holy Spirit, one God, for ever and ever.

Wedding within Mass

Penitential Rite

Let us reflect for a moment on the state of our hearts before God. [Pause] Let us now turn to God, who alone can make our hearts what they are meant to be.

Lord Jesus, you warm our hearts when they are cold, and soften them when they are hard. Lord, have mercy.

You open them when they are closed, and fill them when they are empty. Christ, have mercy.

You heal them when they are wounded, and mend them when they are broken. Lord, have mercy.

May almighty God have mercy on us, forgive us our sins, and bring us to everlasting life.

Opening Prayer

As above

Suggested Reading

C2, p. 133.

Homily

The heart is the universal symbol of love. The human heart is a great repository of love. Sometimes, however, this love remains locked up in our hearts. What is locked up is unused and therefore of no use to anyone. We all need someone who will awaken and open our heart.

When two people fall in love they open their hearts to one another. This opening of the heart happens without any effort on their part. It occurs spontaneously, in the first flush of love.

To open one's heart is a marvellous thing. It is to begin to live. That is why when people fall in love they have an intense feeling of being alive. That's what love does – it brings our hearts to life, and when the heart is alive, we are alive. When two people fall in love, their hearts burst into life like a garden in springtime.

However, to open one's heart is to become vulnerable. When a rosebud opens up to offer its beauty and fragrance to the world, it runs the risk of being plundered and damaged. But consider the alternative. To remain closed up. To remain closed up is never to have lived.

When we open our heart we are leaving ourselves open to being hurt in our softest and most sensitive spot. Our love might not be returned. Worse, it might be betrayed. But what's the alternative? To live with a closed heart. Oscar Wilde says: 'Fear not that your heart might be broken; rather, fear that it might turn into a stone.'

Love is the greatest of all risks. Where there is love, there is pain. In opening our heart we are opening ourselves to pain, but we are also opening ourselves to the possibility of a greater happiness than we have ever known. Love is well-being, and leads to joy. Joy is an overflowing heart.

Most couples go through a honeymoon phase. The honeymoon phase is a pure experience of open heart. It gives a couple a sense of what is possible. However, this phase doesn't last. Many couples get discouraged when the honeymoon period ends and they start to encounter difficulties in each other. As a result, the heart may begin to close and to harden. That would be a disaster. If hardness of heart sets in, it is the beginning of the end.

Each of us has a heart that is capable of love. But to some degree all of us are wounded. The part of us that is most deeply wounded

95

is the heart. We need to heal the wounds of the heart in order to bear the fruits of love.

The greatest anguish of all is the anguish of an empty heart. Sometimes people try to fill the void of the heart with possessions. Only love can fill the heart. Genuine love not only fills the heart but also enlarges it. And when limits are extended or stretched, they tend to stay stretched.

Nothing provides a greater challenge to love, or offers such opportunities for its practice, as marriage. Marriage is rooted and grounded in love. It invites us to open our heart and share its riches. By sharing, our fears disappear, our defences fall away, and our capacity expands and grows.

Human love, however, can never fully satisfy the longings of our hearts. Human love always falls short, but creates in us a longing for complete love. Only God can provide us with complete love. In God all our scattered longings are gathered together. In the memorable words of St Augustine: 'You made us for yourself, O Lord, and our hearts will never rest until they rest in you.'

Prayer of the Faithful

President   Let us now turn to God in prayer, and ask him to take away our hearts of stone and to give us hearts that are warm and loving.

Response   Lord, hear us in your love.

For the followers of Jesus: that the Holy Spirit may kindle in their hearts the fire of his love. [Pause] We pray in faith.

For N. and N.: that their lives may be characterised by love, joy, patience, kindness, and self-control. [Pause] We pray in faith.

That the peace of God, which passes all understanding, may reign in their hearts and in their home. [Pause] We pray in faith.

For all of us: that God may give us warm and compassionate hearts. [Pause] We pray in faith.

For those who have died, especially … (here we could

mention anyone who was related to the bride or groom): that freed from every shadow of death, they may take their place in the new creation where all tears are wiped away. [Pause] We pray in faith.

President: Heavenly Father, fill our hearts with your love. Give us the grace to rise above our human weakness, and keep us faithful to you and to one another. We ask this through Christ our Lord.

Blessing

May you know the joy that springs up in the hearts of those who say 'yes' to love.

May you know the sweetness that falls like dew into the hearts of those who treat others kindly.

And may the Lord bless your home with the laughter of children.

Reflection – SPRINGTIME IN THE HEART

One January day I passed an old cherry tree. It had a bare and forlorn look about it. It contained not a shred of beauty.

I passed the tree again in April. When I looked at it now I could scarcely believe my eyes, so great was the transformation it had undergone in that short interval of time. It was now dressed in a robe of brilliant blossoms.

From where had all this beauty come? The answer was simple.

It had come from within the tree itself. On looking at it back in January, when it was still in the grip of winter, who could have believed that it contained all this? And all this happened as a result of the coming of spring.

Each of us has a capacity for goodness,
but this goodness often remains locked up in our hearts.
We need our hearts to be awakened and opened.
This is what love does.
Love brings our hearts to life.
When two people fall in love,
their heart bursts into life

like a cherry tree in springtime.
This will inevitably result in some pain,
because to open one's heart is to become vulnerable
in one's softest and most sensitive spot.
But there is a worse kind of suffering –
to live with a closed heart,
and to die without having experienced even one spring.

Reflection – THE WOUNDED HEART

If only the heart was right
we could give so much more.
But, alas, the heart is not always right.
It is often empty.
It is often cold and unwelcoming.
It is often hard and unyielding.
It is often weighed down with worry.
It is often sad and lonely.
It is often in darkness.
It is often wounded.
And it is sometimes broken.
We need to heal the wounds of the heart
in order to be able to love.
Lord, open our hearts when they are closed,
soften them when they are hard,
warm them when they are cold,
brighten them when they are dark,
fill them when they are empty,
calm them when they are troubled,
cleanse them when they are sullied,
heal them when they are wounded,
and mend them when they are broken,
so that we, your disciples,
may bear the fruits of love.
Amen.

Wedding Anniversaries

Introduction

We are led to believe that in this day and age to undertake a life-long commitment is, for the majority of people, completely out of the question. Indeed, the impression given is that many people are reluctant even to think about it.

But the fact is, in spite of everything, a great number of married couples still manage to do the unthinkable. They not only undertake the commitment to be faithful to one another for life but actually see it through. But these seldom if ever attract the attention of the media.

Hence, one would expect that the Church would make a fuss over wedding anniversaries. Alas, such is far from being the case, which is a pity. The Church should be seen, not merely to demand lasting fidelity from couples, but to stand by them in carrying it out, encouraging them when they are struggling, and of course rejoicing and celebrating with them when they succeed.

The silver and golden anniversaries are looked upon as the really big milestones of the marriage journey, and normally are the only ones celebrated. But what is so magic about the numbers twenty-five and fifty? Why not, for instance, celebrate fifteen years, or twenty years of faithful love?

Most times it is left to the couple themselves, or to their family, whether or not to mark the occasion. While a celebration cannot be imposed, nevertheless, it could be suggested and encouraged. A parish community could, for instance, invite couples who have been together for a good number of years, and ask them to renew their marriage promises at a public ceremony — a Sunday Mass perhaps? What a wonderful boost this would be for the couples and families involved. What a wonderful example it would be for couples not long married. And what a powerful lesson for young people contemplating marriage.

In what follows, four anniversary liturgies are given. In each case the number of years is left open. However, any of the liturgies in this book could, with a little tailoring, be adapted for such an occasion. Also included is a formula for the renewal of the marriage vows.

The anniversary celebration, done with some solemnity, would provide couples with an opportunity to repeat to one another their vows of lasting love and fidelity. And I'm sure they would be happy to echo the sentiments of the psalmist: 'Not to us, Lord, not to us, but to your name give the glory.' (Ps 115:1).

Renewal of Marriage Vows

This takes place after the homily. All stand.

President   Dear N. and N., on the day of your wedding you declared your love for one another in the presence of the Church's minister and the community. Christ has abundantly blessed your love, and will continue to do so. He consecrated you in baptism, and enriched and strengthened you in the sacrament of matrimony, so that you could carry out the duties of marriage in mutual and lasting fidelity.

   The Church congratulates you and rejoices with you on reaching the .... milestone of your marriage journey. And so on this happy day I invite you to renew your marriage vows.

Husband   N., I renew the commitment I made to you on our wedding day.
   I promise to be true to you in good times and in bad, in sickness and in health.
   I will love you and honour you all the days of my life.

Wife   N., I renew the commitment I made to you on our wedding day.
   I promise to be true to you in good times and in bad, in sickness and in health.
   I will love you and honour you all the days of my life.

President   You have renewed your wedding vows in the presence of the Lord and this community. May the Lord in his goodness deepen your commitment to one another, and fill you both with his blessings.

Husband and wife may now offer one another a sign of love.

The Prayer of the Faithful follows.

14
Remaining faithful

Beatitudes of life
Sow good seed

Introduction

In the name of the Father and of the Son and of the Holy Spirit.

The grace of our Lord Jesus Christ, the love of God, and the fellowship of the Holy Spirit be with you all.

.... years ago (to-day) N. and N. made a solemn promise to be faithful to one another for the rest of their lives. God blessed and sealed their promise, and by his grace has enabled them to remain faithful to it.

We are happy for them, and want to join with them in thanking God for all the graces and blessings he has given them during their married life.

Penitential Rite

All of us have made promises of one kind or another. Let us reflect for a moment on the fact that while it is easy to make a promise, it is not always easy to carry it out. [Pause]

Rare are the people who fully live up to their promises. Let us ask God for forgiveness for our infidelities.

I confess to almighty God ....

Prayers of the Mass
See Roman Missal

Suggested Reading
A6, p. 127.

Homily

Peter had an orchard which produced excellent apples. One spring, in a burst of generosity, he promised to give some apples to his good friend, Paul. So when autumn came around he filled a sack with apples, and on a bright morning put the sack on his back, and set out for the house of his friend.

He hadn't gone far when he discovered that the sack was very heavy. Reluctantly he removed a quantity of the apples. This done, he resumed his journey. However, the sack was still heavy and hurting his shoulder. So once again he lightened it. Then he promised himself that there would be no more concessions to his weakness.

But he bargained without considering certain facts. He had forgotten that the house of his friend was all of fifteen miles away. He had also forgotten to bring food with him. At a certain point a gnawing hunger began to torment him. On top of all these difficulties the day was unbearably hot.

He seriously thought about turning back. The thing that kept him going was the promise he had made to his friend. But meantime he needed some relief from his troubles. So it was that he turned to the apples. Some of these he ate. Others he exchanged for food and cigarettes with strangers he met along the way.

When he finally reached the house of his friend, he paused at the gate and looked into the sack. To his horror he discovered that there was only a handful of apples left in it. He was at a loss as to know how to explain this to his friend.

All of us have made promises. While it is easy to make a promise, it is not always easy to carry it out. Like the man with the bag of apples, we learn a number of lessons in attempting to deliver on our promises.

On the day we make a promise we have little or no idea what that promise entails. But as we go on in life, the full implications of it are gradually revealed to us. We learn, too, that we are self-divided. Each of us is a mixture of strength and weakness, courage and cowardice, generosity and selfishness. And we discover the meaning of friendship. Friendship is not just a nice feeling among people who get along well together, but something which calls for a readiness to make sacrifices and undergo pain. Anyone who has made a significant promise can vouch for the truth of these things.

... years ago N. and N. made a very significant promise to one another. They promised to share with one another, not a bag of apples, but the whole of their lives. They vowed to make a gift of their whole selves to one another. They have travelled a long way since then, and no doubt have learned a lot of things.

During those years they have learned what it was they promised each other on their wedding day. They have learned a lot about themselves. And undoubtedly they have learned a lot about love, particularly how costly it can be. Yet, in spite of everything, they are still on the chosen road, and still delivering to one another.

Every promise has to be remade, not once, but many times. This celebration gives them an opportunity to thank God for his fidelity to them, to thank one another, and to remake those solemn promises they made ... years ago.

Renewal of vows takes place now.
See page 100.

Prayer of the Faithful

President   God is always faithful to us. Let us pray that we may be faithful to God and to one another.

Response   Lord, hear our prayer.

Reader(s)   For the followers of Christ: that they may be steadfast in faith, joyful in hope, and untiring in love all the days of their lives. [Pause] Let us pray to the Lord.

For all who hold public office: that they may be faithful to their commitments and responsibilities. [Pause] Let us pray to the Lord.

For N. and N.: that they may persevere on the difficult but joyful path of faithful love. [Pause] Let us pray to the Lord.

For all here present: that God may bless us with a generous and faithful love so that we may be true to our promises. [Pause] Let us pray to the Lord.

For the victims of broken promises: that they may know healing and peace. [Pause] Let us pray to the Lord.

For the faithful departed, especially those near and dear to us: that they may dwell in the house of the Lord for ever. [Pause] Let us pray to the Lord.

President: All-powerful God, grant that what we have said with our lips, we may believe with our hearts, and practise with our lives. We make this prayer through Christ our Lord.

Blessing

May God, the almighty Father, bless you today and for ever.
May the only Son of God help you in good times and in bad.
May the Holy Spirit of God fill your hearts with his love.

Reflection – BEATITUDES OF LIFE

Blessed are the faithful:
they are like safe anchors in a world of broken moorings.
Blessed are the just:
they are to society what leaven is to bread.
Blessed are the generous:

they keep alive our faith in the essential goodness of people.
Blessed are the caring:
they shine like beacons in a world of indifference.
Blessed are the genuine:
they glow like gems in a world of falseness.
Blessed are those who are not afraid of sacrifice:
on the day of the harvest they will sing for joy.
And blessed are those who refuse to look back:
they will be found worthy of the Kingdom of Heaven.

Reflection – SOW GOOD SEED

In general, we reap what we sow.
We can't expect to reap good if we sow evil.
We must sow peace if we do not want to reap conflict.
We must sow loyalty if we not want to reap betrayal.
We must sow honesty if we not want to reap deceit.
Even though we have no absolute guarantee
that what we sow will always fall on good ground,
or that someone else may not come along
and sow contrary seed, nevertheless,
if we are careful to sow good seeds,
we can, within reason, trust our expectations,
because nature has shown,
that if what is planted bears fruit at all,
it will yield more of itself.
Therefore, let us sow good seed.

15
The lamp still burns

Thank you
A prayer for parents

Introduction

In the name of the Father and of the Son and of the Holy Spirit.

The grace and peace of God our Father and the Lord Jesus Christ be with you.

This is a bright day for N. and N., as well as for all of us who are celebrating the occasion with them. What makes this day a bright one is the fact that the lamp of their love, lit … years ago, is still burning. This is a cause for joy and thanksgiving.

Penitential Rite

The lamp of human love is a frail one, and can't always be

depended on. But there is one lamp that never goes out. This is the lamp of God's love for us. God's light shines unfailingly on all of his children, deserving and undeserving. Let us reflect for a moment on this wonderful truth. [Pause]

Let us ask God's forgiveness for the fact that we sometimes allow the lamp of love to grow dim or perhaps even to go out altogether.

I confess to almighty God ...

Prayers of the Mass
See Roman Missal

Suggested Reading
C6, p. 136; E2, p. 139.

Homily

Mother Teresa told how one day in Melbourne, Australia, she came across a poor man whom nobody knew existed. He was living in a basement room which was in a terrible state of neglect. There was no light in the room, and he rarely opened the blinds.

She started to tidy the room. At first he protested, but she went ahead anyway. Under a pile of rubbish she found a beautiful oil lamp. And she said to him, 'You've got a beautiful lamp here. How come you never light it?'

'No one ever comes to see me,' he replied.

'Will you promise to light it if my sisters come to see you?'

'Yes,' he replied. 'If I hear a human voice, I'll light the lamp.'

Two of Mother Teresa's nuns began to visit him. Every time the sisters came he had the lamp lighting. Things gradually improved for him. Then one day he said to them, 'Sisters, thank you very much for all your help. I'll be able to manage on my own from now on. But do me a favour. Tell that first sister who came to see me that the lamp she lit in my life is still burning.'

The lamp she lit in my life is still burning. ... years ago a lamp began to shine in the lives of N. and N. — the lamp of their mutual love. That lamp is still burning, and continues to illuminate their lives, and the lives of all of us.

Thanks to modern technology, it is now possible to have a lamp that never goes out. The human lamp, however, has not changed much over the centuries. It remains frail and vulnerable. It takes effort and sacrifice to keep it burning.

Practically all marriages begin very brightly. But this is part of the problem. They begin with high, even impossible, expectations. We expect our partner to give us continuous friendship. And what happens? Problems arise. Boredom sets in. Disillusionment may rear its ugly head. The net result is that the light begins to grow dim.

I'm sure that over the years N. and N. have had their share of difficulties, disappointments and sorrows. Nevertheless, in spite of everything, the lamp of their love is still burning. This is a cause of joy for them and for us. The greater the difficulties and disappointments that are successfully met, the greater the joy and peace which fidelity brings.

But in the final analysis, only God is fully faithful. In his love for us, God has bound himself to us in a covenant of friendship, a covenant to which he is faithful forever.

God understands our struggles and weaknesses. He pardons our failings. He heals our hearts when they are wounded. He saves the lamp of our love from being extinguished by the winds of selfishness and disillusionment.

N. and N. are no doubt very different people from the people they were on their wedding day. We pray that God will keep them faithful to one another, and help them to remain truly in love with one another. To stay in love means to love each other, not as they once were, but as they are now.

Renewal of vows takes place now.
See page 100.

Prayer of the Faithful

President   Let us pray that the lamp of love, which was lit in the lives of N. and N. …. years ago, will continue to illumine their lives, (the lives of their children), and the lives of all of us.

Response   Lord, hear our prayer.

Reader(s)   For all Christians: that through their good deeds they may cause the light of Christ to shine in a world darkened by indifference and hatred. [Pause] Let us pray to the Lord.

For all those who hold public office: that through their wisdom and integrity they may cause the light of peace to shine on a world darkened by strife and war. [Pause] Let us pray to the Lord.

For N. and N.: that they may continue to walk in the light of a true and faithful love for one another. [Pause] Let us pray to the Lord.

For all of us, married or single: that we may walk in the light of goodness and faithfulness. [Pause] Let us pray to the Lord.

For the faithful departed, especially our own relatives and friends: that the light of heaven may shine on them. [Pause] Let us pray to the Lord.

President: Almighty and ever-loving God, may the radiance of your love light up our hearts, and bring us safely through the shadows of this world until we reach our homeland of everlasting light. We ask this through Christ our Lord.

Blessing

May the Lord bless you and keep you.

May the Lord let his face shine on you, and be gracious to you.

May the Lord look kindly on you and give you peace now and forevermore.

Reflection – THANK YOU

I love you
not only for what you are,
but for what I am when I am with you.
I love you
not only for what you have made of yourself,

but for what you are making of me.
I love you
for the part of me that you bring out;
for passing over the many foolish and weak things
you find in me,
and for drawing out into the light
all the beautiful things only you could find in me.
You have done more for me than any creed.
You have made me feel my own goodness.
And all this you have done
with your touch,
with your words,
with yourself.
Thank you.

Anonymous

Reflection – A PRAYER FOR PARENTS

Lord, grant us children,
who will be strong enough to know when they are weak;
who will be unbending in defeat,
yet humble and gentle in victory.
Grant us children,
whose wishes will not take the place of their deeds;
children who will know You and know themselves.
Lead them, we pray you, not in the path of ease and comfort,
but rather in the path of difficulties and challenges.
Grant us children,
whose hearts will be clear, and whose goals will be high;
children who will master themselves
before seeking to master others.
And after all these things, add, we pray,
a sense of humour, so that they can be serious,
yet never take themselves too seriously.
Then we, their parents, will dare whisper,
we have not lived in vain.

General Douglas Mac Arthur

16
Still on the chosen road

The second call
Importance of family

Introduction

In the name of the Father and of the Son and of the Holy Spirit.

The grace of our Lord Jesus Christ, the love of God, and the fellowship of the Holy Spirit be with you.

.... years ago N. and N. linked their lives together. They vowed that from that day on they would travel the road of life together as husband and wife. Thanks be to God, they are still together. We are happy for them. The whole Church is happy for them.

Penitential Rite

Whether married or single, all of us are on the great and mysterious journey of life, a journey that can never be re-traced. Let us reflect for a moment on where we are in our journey right now. [Pause]

Perhaps we are disappointed, or hurt, or guilty. Let us turn to God who loves each of us as a dear son or daughter, and ask him for pardon, healing, and strength.

Lord, you were sent to heal the broken-hearted. Lord, have mercy.

You came to call sinners to repentance. Christ, have mercy.

You plead for us at the right hand of the Father. Lord, have mercy.

Prayers of the Mass
See Roman Missal

Suggested Reading
A7, p. 127.

Homily

Marriage can be compared to a journey. When a man and woman get married they commit themselves to a common journey. This journey almost invariably begins with great expectations and in a blaze of joy. But what happens? Difficulties arise. Problems occur. Boredom sets in. As a result the partners may become disappointed and perhaps even disillusioned.

However, there is no need to panic. All this is natural, and happens in every walk of life, even in the most sacred professions and vocations. A young doctor on beginning his practice treats his patients as if they were his own children. But pretty soon this changes due to the pressures of the daily grind. A priest celebrates his first Mass with one foot in heaven. But before a year has passed he is well and truly back down to earth.

I believe most couples could identify with this. No doubt, during the past ... years, N. and N. have had their joys and sorrows, satisfactions and disappointments, successes and failures. Their journey may have been more difficult than they had envisaged.

A difficult journey is not necessarily a misfortune. In fact it can turn out to be a blessing. The very difficulties N. and N. have encountered and overcome, the sacrifices they have made for each other, far from loosening the bond with which they linked their lives on their wedding day, have had the effect of strengthening it.

N. and N. have reached the ... milestone of their common journey. We are happy for them. The Church is happy for them and congratulates them. This happy occasion provides them with an opportunity to renew their vows to one another. Every choice in life has to be re-made, not once, but many times. Each day a new part of the chosen path opens up before us. We have to say 'yes' to the new as we said 'yes' to the old.

As we proceed along the path of life, the full implications of our original choice are gradually revealed to us. Hence, we have to go on repeating and renewing that original 'yes' we said all those years ago.

This occasion is also an opportunity for N. and N. to let go of any unnecessary baggage they may have picked up along the way — regrets for what might have been, bitterness over hurts suffered, guilt over mistakes made, and so on.

Gratitude for what they have been able to achieve, forgiveness for what has gone wrong—these will help them to go forward with renewed spirit. Fidelity brings its own rewards in terms of peace and happiness.

We pray that God will help them to persevere in the path of faithful love, and that their relationship will go on deepening.

Renewal of vows takes place now.
See page 100.

Prayer of the Faithful

President   It is from God we come when we enter this world, and it is to God we go when we leave it. Let us ask for his guidance and grace so that we may walk more readily in his ways.

Response   Lord, hear us in your love.

Reader(s)   For all Christians: that they may follow Christ with steadfastness and generosity. [Pause] We pray in faith.

For all government leaders: that they may work to build a world free from war and hunger, so that all people may be able to live in freedom and dignity. [Pause] We pray in faith.

For N. and N.: that the journey they began ... years ago may continue in faith, hope and love. [Pause] We pray in faith.

For all here present: that we may draw inspiration for our own journey from our participation in this celebration. [Pause] We pray in faith.

For all our departed relatives and friends: that God may bring them into his kingdom of light and peace. [Pause] We pray in faith.

President   God of love and mercy, grant us in all our tasks your help, in all our doubts your guidance, in all our weaknesses your strength, in all our sorrows your consolation, and in all our dangers your protection. We ask this through Christ our Lord.

Blessing

May the Lord guide you in the way of love, and fill your both with Christlike patience.

May the Lord enable you to walk in newness of life, and to please him in all things.

May you walk in innocence of heart so that you may know the joy of the upright.

Reflection – THE SECOND CALL

In theory a calling would appear to be a very straight-forward thing. One hears the call clearly and responds to it whole-heartedly.

But in reality it's never that simple.

There are two calls of Peter related in the Gospels. The first occurred at the start of Jesus' ministry. (See Mark 1:16-18). This call was rather brief and informal, and was addressed not only to Peter but also to his brother, Andrew. Jesus said, 'Follow me and I will make you fishers of men.' And Peter dropped everything and followed Jesus.

Yet that first call ended in disaster. In the garden of Gethsemane, when Jesus needed Peter's support, he wasn't there for him; he was sleeping. Worse was to follow. Later that night he denied that he had ever known Jesus.

Why didn't Jesus discarded Peter as being weak, cowardly, and unreliable? Because he knew there was another and better side to Peter. In spite of his weakness, his heart was sound. So Jesus did not discard him. Instead, he called him a second time.

The second call occurred after the resurrection. (See John 21:1-19). This call was more personal because it was addressed to Peter alone. Three times Jesus said to him, 'Peter, do you love me?' And Peter said, 'Lord, you know that I love you.'

Three years separated those two calls. During that time a lot had happened in Peter's life. He had grown in knowledge of Jesus. He had grown in understanding of the mission to which Jesus had called him. And he had grown in self-knowledge. When the second call came, he was a humbler and wiser man. Hence, the 'yes' he pronounced this time was a more mature and enlightened one.

Jesus restored Peter to where he was before, and made him the chief shepherd of his flock. And this time Peter did not fail him. It was he who led the apostles in witnessing to the resurrection.

Peter is a great challenge to us; he had the guts to get again after his fall. But he is also a great consolation to us, because courage fails us all. We must learn to forgive ourselves. And we must not judge ourselves or others by momentary lapses, but by commitment given over a long time.

Peter's story shows that call doesn't exclude falls. A call is not something we hear once and answer once. A call has to be heard many times, and responded to many times. Each day a new part of the chosen path opens up before us. We have to say 'yes' to the new as we have said 'yes' to the old.

We all need someone to believe in us, and who doesn't write us off because we don't come up with the goods all at once.

Reflection – IMPORTANCE OF FAMILY

Of all the influences upon us,
the family is the most powerful.
Here is where we put down our roots.
What we draw in through those roots
will nourish or poison us for the rest of our lives.
Every family is a small community.
The virtues that build and foster community are:
kindness, gentleness, patience,
humility, mutual forgiveness, and love.
These are not easy virtues to practise.
But when practised with consistency,
the rewards are great
in terms of peace and harmony in the home.

17
The bond still holds

Handicaps of the normal
Trust in God

Introduction

In the name of the Father and of the Son and of the Holy Spirit.

The grace and peace of God our Father and the Lord Jesus Christ be with you.

… years ago N. and N. tied the knot, as we say. They bound their lives and destinies together. And by the grace of God, and their co-operation with that grace, the bond still holds.

We are celebrating this Mass to thank God for the graces he has given them during the past … years, and also for the example of faithfulness they have given us.

Penitential Rite

In one way or another, all our lives are bound together, so much so that we have a profound influence on one another for good or ill. Let us reflect on this for a moment. [Pause]

We are not always as helpful or as loyal to one another as we could be. Therefore, let us ask forgiveness from God and from one another .

I confess to almighty God …

Prayers of the Mass
See Roman Missal

Suggested Reading
A4, p. 127

Homily

… years ago N. and N. bound their lives together in the sacrament of marriage. The bond of marriage is not meant to be a mere legal tie. Nor is it meant to be a fetter, making prisoners of the partners. It is meant to be a bond of love. The thing which creates a bond of love between people is sacrifice.

Only that man understands what a farm is who has sacrificed part of himself to that farm. This sacrifice creates a bond between him and his farm. Only that woman understands what a home is who has worked to make it beautiful. It is precisely because of the sacrifices she has made for her home that the love of it fills her heart. In the same way, only that couple who have sacrificed themselves for one another understand what marriage is. For them the marriage bond is truly a bond of love.

Alexander Solzhenitsyn, the Russian writer, experienced war and imprisonment for his country. But he tells how this experience, far from impoverishing him, greatly enriched him. 'I must admit,' he says, 'that before my experience of war and prison I didn't have much faith in friends, particularly in the business of laying down one's life for them. But the war changed all this. During the war we drank to friendship and love. In roadside ditches, in flooded trenches, in the ruins of gutted houses we learned the value of a tin of soup, an hour of quiet, the meaning of true friendship, the meaning of life itself.'

But he goes on to say that on returning to civilian life he and his fellow soldiers were stunned by what they found. They were appalled by the callous, often totally unscrupulous way in which people treated one another.

It is not an easy life but a difficult life which creates a deep bond between people. The very difficulties encountered, and the sacrifices made for one another, are what fashion and strengthen the bond between them. These are precisely the things out of which friendship and loyalty are born.

During the past … years no doubt N. and N. have had their ups and downs, joys and sorrows, successes and failures, satisfactions and disappointments. They have travelled a long way and been through a lot together. Yet, by the grace of God and their co-operation with that grace, the bond by which they linked their lives together on their wedding day has held. We pray that the problems they have overcome together, and the sacrifices they have made for one another, will strengthen that bond.

This ceremony gives them an opportunity to commit themselves once more to one another. God blessed them on their wedding day. God blesses them again today. May they go forward in confidence, knowing that his grace will keep them faithful in the future as it did in the past.

Renewal of vows takes place now.
See page 100.

Prayer of the Faithful

President   Left to ourselves, we cannot do the will of God. Therefore, let us turn to God with confidence, and ask him to guide our wayward hearts.

Response   Lord, graciously hear us.

Reader(s)   For the Church: that God may bind its members together in unity and peace so that the world will know that they are disciples of Jesus. [Pause] Lord, hear us.

For world leaders: that God may bless them with wisdom and integrity so that they may bind the human family together in ties of friendship and co-operation. [Pause] Lord, hear us.

For N. and N.: that God may bless them today, and strengthen the bond by which their lives and destinies are joined together. [Pause] Lord, hear us.

For marriages that have broken down: that God may heal the wounds which result from every breakdown. [Pause] Lord, hear us.

For all gathered here: that we may draw inspiration for our own lives from this celebration. [Pause] Lord, hear us.

For those whom we loved in this life, but whom death has taken from us: that God may bring them to a place of refreshment, light, and peace. [Pause] Lord hear us.

President   Heavenly Father, fill our hearts with your love. Give us the grace to rise above our human weaknesses, and keep us faithful to you and to one another. We ask this through Christ our Lord.

Blessing

May you know the happiness of those who walk in faithful love.
May you live in such a way that your lives will be an example for others.
And may the God of love, who brought you together,
hold you both in the hollow of his hand.

Reflection – HANDICAPS OF THE NORMAL

Each of us has an innate capacity to love.
Unfortunately, this love often lies unexpressed.
Why is this?
Because all of us are handicapped in one way or another.
We have hands and we don't give,
eyes and we don't see,

ears and we don't hear,
tongues and we don't speak,
feelings and we don't show them.
The greatest handicap of all, however, is a crippled heart.
A paraplegic observed:
'Living as a cripple in a wheelchair allows you
to see more clearly the crippled hearts of some people
whose bodies are whole and whose minds are sound.'
Hence, each of us stands in daily need of a conversion
from a closed heart to an open heart,
from a heart of stone to a heart of flesh.
When all is said and done it is the heart that matters.
To close one's heart is to begin to die.
To open one's heart is to begin to live.

Reflection – TRUST IN GOD

Those who trust in God are truly blessed;
God himself becomes their strength.
They are like a tree planted by the waterside,
sending out its roots to the stream.
It has no worries in time of drought;
its foliage stays green,
and it never ceases to bear fruit.
Lord, give us the kind of trust in you
that will sustain us in times of difficulty,
that will make our lives fruitful,
and that will keep our hope unfading.
Amen.

Scripture Readings

A

Old Testament readings

Note All the Scripture readings are set out in such a way as to make the reader's task easier.

Scriptural Note Genesis has two accounts of the institution of marriage. The first (1:26-28) sees marriage as a means of procreation. The second (2:18-24) sees marriage as meeting the human need for companionship.

A1   Genesis 1:26-28.31
God made man and woman for one another. The bond of marriage means that they are no longer two but one.

A Reading from the Book of Genesis
Then God said:
'Let us make humankind in our image, according to our like-
    ness; and let them have dominion over the fish of the sea,
and over the birds of the air,
and over the cattle,
and over all the wild animals of the earth,
and over every creeping thing that creeps upon the earth.'
So God created humankind in his own image,
in the image of God he created them;
male and female he created them.
God blessed them, and God said to them,
'Be fruitful and multiply, and fill the earth and subdue it;
and have dominion over the fish of the sea
and over the birds of the air
and over every living thing that moves upon the earth.'

God saw everything that he had made,
and indeed, it was very good. [Pause]
This is the word of the Lord.

A2   Genesis 2:18-24

In and through marriage, God intends man and woman to be
partners and companions.

A reading from the Book of Genesis

Then the Lord God said:
'It is not good that the man should be alone;
I will make him a helper as his partner.'
So out of the ground the Lord God formed
every animal of the field and every bird of the air,
and brought them to the man to see what he would call them;
and whatever the man called every living creature,
that was its name.
The man gave names to all cattle,
to the birds of the air, and to every animal of the field;
but for the man there was not found a helper as his partner.
So the Lord God caused a deep sleep to fall upon the man,
and while he slept,
he took one of his ribs and closed up its place with flesh.
And the rib which the Lord God had taken from the man
he made into a woman and brought her to the man.
Then the man said:
'This at last is bone of my bones and flesh of my flesh;
this one shall be called Woman,
for out of Man this one was taken.'
Therefore a man leaves his father and his mother
and clings to his wife, and they become one flesh. [Pause]
This is the word of the Lord.

A3   Tobit 8:4-9

This is a prayer made by Tobit and his spouse, Sarah. It is one which
any married couple could make their own.

A reading from the book of Tobit

Tobias got out of bed and said to Sarah,
'Sister, get up, and let us pray and implore our Lord
that he grant us mercy and safety.'
So she got up, and they began to pray
that they might be kept safe.
Tobias began by saying:
'Blessed are you, O God of our ancestors,
and blessed is your name in all generations forever.
Let the heavens and the whole creation bless you forever.
You made Adam, and for him you made his wife Eve
as a helper and support.
From the two of them the human race has sprung.
You said: "It's not good that the man should be alone;
let us make a helper for him like himself."
I now am taking this kinswoman of mine,
not because of lust, but with sincerity.
Grant that she and I may find mercy
and that we may grow old together.'
And they both said, 'Amen, Amen.' [Pause]
This is the word of the Lord.

A4   Sirach 6:6-12.14-15

This reading stresses the value of a true friend.

A Reading from the Book of Sirach

Let those who are friendly with you be many,
but let your advisers be one in a thousand.
When you gain friends, gain them through testing,
and do not trust them hastily.
For there are friends who are such when it suits them,
but they will not stand by you in time of trouble.
And there are friends who change into enemies,
and tell of the quarrel to your disgrace.
And there are friends who sit at your table,
but they will not stand by you in time of trouble.
When you are prosperous,
they become your second self, and lord it over your servants;

but if you are brought low,
they turn against you, and hide themselves from you.
Faithful friends are a sturdy shelter:
whoever finds one has found a treasure.
Faithful friends are beyond price;
no amount can balance their worth. [Pause]
This is the word of the Lord.

A5   Song of Songs 2:10-14.16; 8:6-7

This is a poem in praise of love.

A reading from the Song of Songs

My beloved speaks and says to me:
'Arise, my love, my fair one, and come away;
for now the winter is past,
the rain is over and gone.
The flowers appear on the earth;
the time of singing has come,
and the voice of the turtle-dove is heard in our land.
The fig tree puts forth its figs,
and the vines are in blossom;
they give forth fragrance.
Arise, my love, my fair one, and come away.
Let me see your face,
let me hear your voice;
for your voice is sweet,
and your face is lovely.'
My beloved is mine and I am his.
He said to me:
'Set me as a seal upon your heart,
as a seal upon your arm;
for love is strong as death.
Many waters cannot quench love,
neither can floods drown it.
If a man offered for love all the wealth of his house,
it would be utterly scorned.' [Pause]
This is the word of the Lord.

A6 Isaiah 54:4-5.9-10

God has made an everlasting covenant with us. The marriage covenant is a reflection of this.

> A reading from the prophet Isaiah
>
> Do not fear, for you will not be ashamed;
> do not be discouraged, for you will not suffer disgrace.
> For your Maker is your husband,
> the Lord of hosts is his name;
> and the Holy One of Israel is your Redeemer,
> the God of the whole earth he is called.
> With everlasting love I will have compassion on you,
> says the Lord, your Redeemer.
> This is like the days of Noah to me:
> Just as I swore that the waters of Noah
> would never again go over the earth,
> so I have sworn that I will not be angry with you
> and will not rebuke you.
> For the mountains may depart
> and the hills be removed,
> but my steadfast love shall not depart from you,
> and my covenant of peace shall not be removed,
> says the Lord, who has compassion on you. [Pause]
> This is the word of the Lord.

A7 Ruth 1:16-17

This reading illustrates the bond that marriage forges between two people.

> A reading from the book of Ruth
>
> Ruth said:
> 'Do not press me to leave you
> or to turn back from following you.
> Where you go, I will go;
> Where you live, I will live.
> Your people will be my people,
> and your God will be my God.
> Where you die, I will die,

127

and there I will be buried.
I solemnly declare before the Lord
that nothing but death will part me from you.' [Pause]
This is the word of the Lord.

B

Responsorial psalms

B1   Ps 144 (145):8-11,14,17-18

Response   The Lord is compassionate to all his creatures.

The Lord is kind and full of compassion,
slow to anger, abounding in love.
How good is the Lord to all,
compassionate to all his creatures. *R*

The Lord is faithful in all his words
and loving in all his deeds.
The Lord supports all who fall
and raises all who are bowed down. *R*

The Lord is just in all his ways
and loving in all his deeds.
He is close to all who call him,
who call on him from their hearts. *R*

B2   Ps 120(121):1-8

Response   My help shall come from the Lord
who made heaven and earth

I lift up my eyes to the mountains:
from where shall come my help?
My help shall come from the Lord
who made heaven and earth. *R*

May he never allow you to stumble.
Let him sleep not, your guard.

No, he sleeps not nor slumbers,
Israel's guard. *R*

The Lord is your guard and your shade;
at your right side he stands.
By day the sun shall not smite you
nor the moon in the night. *R*

The Lord will guard you from evil,
he will guard your soul.
The Lord will guard your going and coming
both now and for ever. *R*

B3   Ps 26(27):1,4,10,13,14.

Response   The Lord is my light and my help.

The Lord is my light and my help;
whom, shall I fear?
The Lord is the stronghold of my life;
before whom shall I shrink? *R*

There is one thing I ask of the Lord,
for this I long,
to live in the house of the Lord
all the days of my life. *R*

Do not abandon or forsake me,
O God my help.
Though father and mother forsake me,
the Lord will receive me. *R*

I am sure I shall see the Lord's goodness
in the land of the living.
Hope in him, hold firm and take heart.
Hope in the Lord. *R*

B4   Ps 99(100):1-5

Response   The Lord is faithful from age to age.

Cry out with joy to the Lord, all the earth.
Serve the Lord with gladness.

Come before him, singing for joy. *R*
Know that he, the Lord, is God.
He made us, we belong to him,
we are his people, the sheep of his flock. *R*

Go within his gates, giving thanks.
Enter his courts with songs of praise.
Give thanks to him and bless his name. *R*

Indeed, how good is the Lord,
eternal his merciful love.
He is faithful from age to age. *R*

B5   Ps 91(92):2-6,13-16

Response   It is good to give thanks to the Lord.

It is good to give thanks to the Lord
to make music to your name, O Most High,
to proclaim your love in the morning
and your truth in the watches of the night. *R*

Your deeds, O Lord, have made me glad;
for the work of your hands I shout with joy.
O Lord, how great are your works,
how deep are your designs. *R*

The just will flourish like the palm-tree
and grow like a Lebanon cedar.
Planted in the House of the Lord
they will flourish in the courts of our God. *R*

Still bearing fruit when they are old,
still full of sap, still green,
to proclaim that the Lord is just;
in him, my rock, there is no wrong. *R*

B6   Ps 32(33):12-15,18-22

Response   May your love be upon us, O Lord,
                as we place all our hope in you.

They are happy, whose God is the Lord,
the people he has chosen as his own.
From the heavens the Lord looks forth,
he sees all the children of men. *R*

From the place where he dwells he gazes
on all the dwellers on the earth,
he who shapes the hearts of them all
and considers all their deeds. *R*

The Lord looks on those who revere him,
on those who hope in his love,
to rescue their souls from death,
to keep them alive in famine. *R*

Our soul is waiting for the Lord.
The Lord is our help and our shield.
In him do our hearts find joy.
We trust in his holy name. *R*

B7   Ps 137(138):1-3,6-7

Response   Your love, O Lord, is eternal.

I thank you, Lord, with all my heart,
you have heard the words of my mouth.
Before the angels I will bless you.
I will adore before your holy temple. *R*

I thank you for your faithfulness and love
which excel all we ever knew of you.
On the day I called, you answered;
you increased the strength of my soul. *R*

The Lord is high yet he looks on the lowly
and the haughty he knows from afar.
Though I walk in the midst of affliction
you give me life and frustrate my foes. *R*

You stretch out your hand and save me,
your hand will do all things for me.
Your love, O Lord, is eternal,
discard not the work of your hands. *R*

B8 Ps 102(103):8,10-14,17-18

Response The Lord is compassion and love.

The Lord is compassion and love,
slow to anger and rich in mercy.
He does not treat us according to our sins
nor repay us according to our faults. *R*

For as the heavens are high above the earth
so strong is his love for those who fear him.
As far as the east is from the west
so far does he remove our sins. *R*

As a father has compassion on his children,
the Lord has pity on those who fear him;
for he knows of what we are made,
he remembers that we are dust. *R*

The love of the Lord is everlasting
upon those who fear him;
his justice reaches out to children's children
when they keep his covenant in truth. *R*

C

New Testament readings

C1 Romans 8:31-32.35.37-39

Because God loves us and always takes our side, we are able to
overcome every trial and suffering.

A reading from the letter of St Paul to the Romans

If God is for us, who is against us?
He did not spare his own Son,
but gave him up for all of us.
Will he not with him also give us everything else?
Who shall separate us from the love of Christ?
Will hardship, or distress, or persecution,
or famine, or nakedness, or peril, or sword?

No, in all these things we are more than conquerors
through him who loved us.
For I am convinced that neither death, nor life,
nor angels, nor rulers,
nor things present, nor things to come,
nor powers, nor height, nor depth,
nor anything else in all creation,
will be able to separate us from the love of God
in Christ Jesus our Lord. [Pause]
This is the word of the Lord.

C2   1 Corinthians 13:1-7

No one has so stressed the importance of love, or described it better,
than St Paul

A reading from the first letter of St Paul to the Corinthians

If I speak in the tongues of men and of angels,
but do not have love,
I am a noisy gong or a clanging cymbal.
And if I have prophetic powers,
and understand all mysteries and all knowledge,
and if I have all faith, so as to remove mountains,
but do not have love, I am nothing.
If I give away all my possessions,
and if I hand over my body to be burned,
but do not have love, I gain nothing.
Love is patient; love is kind;
love is not envious or boastful or arrogant or rude.
It does not insist on its own way;
it is not irritable or resentful;
it does not rejoice in wrongdoing, but rejoices in the truth.
It bears all things,
believes all things,
hopes all things,
endures all things.
Love never ends. [Pause]
This is the word of the Lord.

C3   Philippians 4:4-9

This reading tells us how to live in peace with God and with one another.

A reading from the letter of St Paul to the Philippians

Rejoice in the Lord always; again I say, Rejoice.
Let your gentleness be known to everyone.
The Lord is near.
Do not worry about anything,
   but in everything, by prayer and supplication with thanksgiving, let your requests be made known to God.
   And the peace of God, which surpasses all understanding,
   will guard your hearts and your minds in Christ Jesus.
Finally, brothers and sisters,
   whatever is true,
   whatever is honourable,
   whatever is just,
   whatever is pure,
   whatever is pleasing,
   whatever is commendable,
   if there is any excellence
   and if there is anything worthy of praise,
   think about these things.
Keep on doing the things that you have learned and received
   and heard and seen in me,
   and the God of peace will be with you. [Pause]
This is the word of the Lord.

C4   Colossians 3:12-15

These are the virtues which build and foster a relationship.

A reading from the letter of St Paul to the Colossians

As God's chosen ones, holy and beloved,
clothe yourselves with compassion, kindness,
humility, gentleness, and patience.
Bear with one another,
   and if anyone has a complaint against another,
   forgive each other;

just as the Lord has forgiven you,
so you also must forgive.
Above all, clothe yourselves with love,
which binds everything together in perfect harmony.
And let the peace of Christ reign in your hearts. [Pause]
This is the word of the Lord.

C5   Ephesians 4:1-3.25-27.31-32; Romans 12: 2.
These are the virtues which should characterise a Christian marriage.

A reading from St Paul.

I urge you to lead a life worthy of your calling.
Do not model yourselves
on the behaviour of the world around you.
But seek to follow what is right,
and to do the will of God.
Let your love for each other not be a pretence.
Be tolerant with one another,
in complete selflessness, gentleness, and patience.
Do all you can to preserve unity
by the peace that binds you together.
Speak the truth to one another.
Even if you are angry,
do not let the sun go down on your anger
or else you will give evil a foothold.
Do not bear grudges against one another
or allow any sort of spitefulness to grow between you.
Rather, be friends with one another,
and be kind to one another,
forgiving each other
as readily as God forgave you in Christ.
Have a profound respect for one another.
Do not give up if trials come,
and keep on praying. [Pause]
This is the word of the Lord.

C6   1 John 2:7-10

To love is to walk in the light; not to love is to walk in darkness.

A reading from the first letter of St John

Beloved, I am writing you no new commandment,
but an old commandment that you had from the beginning;
the old commandment is the word that you have heard.
Yet I am writing you a new commandment
that is true in him and in you,
because the darkness is passing away
and the true light is already shining.
Whoever says, 'I am in the light,'
while hating a brother or sister,
is still in darkness.
Whoever loves a brother or sister lives in the light,
and in such a person there is no cause for stumbling. [Pause]
This is the word of the Lord.

C7   1 John 4:7-12

Those who love know God because God is love.

A reading from the first letter of Saint John

Beloved, let us love one another, because love is of God;
everyone who loves is born of God and knows God.
Whoever does not love, does not know God, for God is love.
God's love was revealed among us in this way:
God sent his only Son into the world
so that we might live through him.
In this is love,
not that we loved God, but that he loved us,
and sent his Son to be the atoning sacrifice for our sins.
Beloved, since God loved us so much,
we also ought to love one another.
No one has ever seen God;
if we love one another, God lives in us,
and his love is perfected in us. [Pause]
This is the word of the Lord.

D
Gospel acclamations

D1   John 13:34

Alleluia, alleluia! (*Lent:* Praise to you, Lord Jesus Christ).
I give you a new commandment,
that you love one another,
just as I have loved you,
says the Lord.
Alleluia! (*Lent:* Praise to you, Lord Jesus Christ).

D2   John 13:35

Alleluia, alleluia! (*Lent:* Praise to you, Lord Jesus Christ).
By this everyone will know that you are my disciples,
if you have love for one another,
says the Lord.
Alleluia! (*Lent:* Praise to you, Lord Jesus Christ).

D3   John 15:9

Alleluia, alleluia! (*Lent:* Praise to you, Lord Jesus Christ).
As the Father has loved me,
so I have loved you;
abide in my love,
says the Lord.
Alleluia! (*Lent:* Praise to you, Lord Jesus Christ).

D4   John 15:12

Alleluia, alleluia! (*Lent:* Praise to you, Lord Jesus Christ).
This is my commandment,
that you love one another as I have loved you,
says the Lord.
Alleluia! (*Lent:* Praise to you, Lord Jesus Christ).

D5   John 15:13

Alleluia, alleluia! (*Lent:* Praise to you, Lord Jesus Christ).
No one has greater love than this,
to lay down one's life for one's friends.
Alleluia! (*Lent:* Praise to you, Lord Jesus Christ).

D6   1 John 4:7-8
Alleluia, alleluia! (*Lent:* Praise to you, Lord Jesus Christ).
Let us love one another,
because love is from God;
everyone who loves is born of God and knows God,
for God is love.
Alleluia! (*Lent:* Praise to you, Lord Jesus Christ).

E

Gospels

E1   Matthew 5:1-10
Jesus describes the qualities he wishes to see in his followers. A
marriage that is characterised by these qualities will be truly
blessed.

A reading from the holy Gospel according to Matthew

When Jesus saw the crowds, he went up the mountain;
and after he sat down, his disciples came to him.
Then he began to speak, and taught them, saying:
'Blessed are the poor in spirit, for theirs is the kingdom of
      heaven.
Blessed are those who mourn, for they will be comforted.
Blessed are the gentle, for they will inherit the earth.
'Blessed are those who hunger and thirst for righteousness,
for they will be filled.
Blessed are the merciful, for they will receive mercy.
Blessed are the pure in heart, for they will see God.
'Blessed are the peacemakers,
for they will be called children of God.
Blessed are those who are persecuted in the cause of right,
for theirs is the kingdom of heaven.' [Pause]
This is the Gospel of the Lord.

E2   Matthew 5:13-16

Jesus urged his followers to let the light of their good deeds shine for all to see. Every married couple is called to let the light of faithful love shine in a world.

A reading from the holy Gospel according to Matthew

Jesus said to his disciples:
'You are the salt of the earth;
but if salt has lost its taste, how can its saltiness be restored?
It is no longer good for anything,
but is thrown out and trampled under foot.
'You are the light of the world.
A city built on a hill cannot be hid.
No one lights a lamp and puts it under a bushel basket;
they put it on a lamp stand,
so that it gives light to all in the house.
In the same way,
let your light shine before others,
so that they may see your good works
and give glory to your Father in heaven.' [Pause]
This is the Gospel of the Lord.

E3   Matthew 7:21.24-27

Christ made a wonderful promise to those who listen to his teaching and act on it.

A reading from the holy Gospel according to Matthew

Jesus said to his disciples:
'Not everyone who says to me, 'Lord, Lord,'
will enter the kingdom of heaven,
but only the one who does the will of my Father who is in heaven.
Everyone then who hears these words of mine
and acts on them,
will be like a wise man who built his house on rock.
The rain fell,
the floods came,
and the winds blew and beat on that house,

but it did not fall,
because it had been founded on the rock.
And everyone who hears these words of mine
and does not act on them,
will be like a foolish man who built his house on the sand.
The rain fell,
the floods came,
and the winds blew and beat against that house,
and it fell – and great was its fall.' [Pause]
This is the Gospel of the Lord.

E4   Matthew 19:3-6

Christ teaches that the bond of marriage owes it origin to God and
is therefore indissoluble.

A reading from the holy Gospel according to Matthew

Some Pharisees came to Jesus, and to test him they asked,
'Is it lawful for a man to divorce his wife for any cause?'
And he answered,
'Have you not read that the one who made them at the begin-
    ning, made them male and female, and said,
"For this reason a man shall leave his father and mother
and be joined to his wife,
and the two shall become one flesh."
So they are no longer two, but one flesh.
Therefore what God has joined together,
let no one separate.' [Pause]
This is the Gospel of the Lord.

Scripture Note on Matthew 19:3-6

On the basis of Deuteronomy 24:1-4, the Pharisees allowed a husband to divorce his wife because of 'an indecency in her'. Appeal-
ing to Genesis 1:27;2:24, Jesus stressed the unity created by marriage, which would forbid breaking the marriage bond, so that
remarriage after a divorce would constitute adultery.

Jesus is describing the ideal marital relationship, which in its
indissoluble fidelity, mirrors the covenant between God and his
people. But this doesn't mean he wasn't aware of, and sympathetic

towards, the problems that can arise in the living out of that ideal.

Indissoluble monogamy is not just a clerical hobby-horse, but finds a powerful justification in the special needs children have to be nurtured and cared for over a much longer period of time than almost any other member of the animal species.

E5   John 2:1-11

Jesus performed his first miracle at a wedding when he changed water into wine.

A reading from the holy Gospel according to John

There was a marriage in Cana of Galilee,
and the mother of Jesus was there.
Jesus and his disciples had also been invited to the wedding.
When the wine gave out, the mother of Jesus said to him,
'They have no wine.'
And Jesus said to her,
'Woman, what concern is that to you and to me?
My hour has not yet come.'
His mother said to the servants,
'Do whatever he tells you.'
Now standing there were six stone jars
for the Jewish rites of purification,
each holding twenty or thirty gallons.
Jesus said to the servants, 'Fill the jars with water.'
And they filled them up to the brim.
Then he said to them,
'Now draw some out, and take it to the chief steward.'
So they took it.
When the steward tasted the water that had become wine,
and did not know where it came from,
(though the servants who had drawn the water knew),
the steward called the bridegroom and said to him,
'Everyone serves the good wine first,
and then the inferior wine after the guests have become drunk.
But you have kept the good wine until now.'
Jesus did this, the first of his signs, in Cana of Galilee,
and revealed his glory;

and his disciples believed in him. [Pause]
This is the Gospel of the Lord.

E6   John 15:9-12; 13:35
Jesus urges his disciples to love one another as he has loved them.

A reading from the holy Gospel according to John.

Jesus said to his disciples:
'As the Father has loved me, so I have loved you;
abide in my love.
If you keep my commandments,
you will abide in my love,
just as I have kept my Father's commandments
and abide in his love.
I have said these things to you,
so that my joy may be in you,
and that your joy may be complete.
This is my commandment,
that you love one another as I have loved you.
By this everyone will know that you are my disciples,
if you have love for one another.' [Pause]
This is the Gospel of the Lord.